THE WAY
PEOPLE
LIVE

Life in the Hitler Youth

Titles in The Way People Live series include:

THE WAY
PEOPLE
LIVE

Life in the Hitler Youth

by Jennifer Keeley

Lucent Books, P.O. Box 289011, San Diego, CA 92198-9011

Library of Congress Cataloging-in-Publication Data

Keeley, Jennifer, 1974–
     Life in the Hitler Youth / by Jennifer Keeley.
          p.   cm. — (The way people live)
     Includes bibliographical references and index.
     Summary: Discusses life among the Hitler Youth, including their ideology
and activities, school and home life, and involvement in World War II.
     ISBN 1-56006-613-X (alk. paper)
     1. Hitler-Jugend—Juvenile literature.   2. National socialism—Juvenile
literature.   3. Youth—Germany—Societies and clubs—Juvenile literature.
4. Germany—Politics and government—1933–1945—Juvenile literature.
[1. Hitler Youth. 2. National socialism. 3. Germany—Politics and government
—1933–1945.]
     I. Title.   II. Series.
     DD253.5.K34   2000
     943.086'0835—dc21   99-37017
                                                                                        CIP

Contents

Discovering the Humanity in Us All

Books in The Way People Live series focus on groups of people in a wide variety of circumstances, settings, and time periods. Some books focus on different cultural groups, others, on people in a particular historical time period, while others cover people involved in a specific event. Each book emphasizes the daily routines, personal and historical struggles, and achievements of people from all walks of life.

To really understand any culture, it is necessary to strip the mind of the common notions we hold about groups of people. These stereotypes are the archenemies of learning. It does not even matter whether the stereotypes are positive or negative; they are confining and tight. Removing them is a challenge that's not easily met, as anyone who has ever tried it will admit. Ideas that do not fit into the templates we create are unwelcome visitors—ones we would prefer remain quietly in a corner or forgotten room.

The cowboy of the Old West is a good example of such confining roles. The cowboy was courageous, yet soft-spoken. His time (it is always a he, in our template) was spent alternatively saving a rancher's daughter from certain death on a runaway stagecoach, or shooting it out with rustlers. At times, of course, he was likely to get a little crazy in town after a trail drive, but for the most part, he was the epitome of inner strength. It is disconcerting to find out that the cowboy is human, even a bit childish. Can it really be true that cowboys would line up to help the cook on the trail drive grind coffee, just hoping he would give them a little stick of peppermint candy that came with the coffee shipment? The idea of tough cowboys vying with one another to help "Coosie" (as they called their cooks) for a bit of candy seems silly and out of place.

So is the vision of Eskimos playing video games and watching MTV, living in prefab housing in the Arctic. It just does not fit with what "Eskimo" means. We are far more comfortable with snow igloos and whale blubber, harpoons and kayaks.

Although the cultures dealt with in Lucent's The Way People Live series are often historically and socially well known, the emphasis is on the personal aspects of life. Groups of people, while unquestionably affected by their politics and their governmental structures, are more than those institutions. How do people in a particular time and place educate their children? What do they eat? And how do they build their houses? What kinds of work do they do? What kinds of games do they enjoy? The answers to these questions bring these cultures to life. People's lives are revealed in the particulars and only by knowing the particulars can we understand these cultures' will to survive and their moments of weakness and greatness.

This is not to say that understanding politics does not help to understand a culture. There is no question that the Warsaw ghetto, for example, was a culture that was brought about by the politics and social ideas of Adolf

Hitler and the Third Reich. But the Jews who were crowded together in the ghetto cannot be understood by the Reich's politics. Their life was a day-to-day battle for existence, and the creativity and methods they used to prolong their lives is a vital story of human perseverance that would be denied by focusing only on the institutions of Hitler's Germany. Knowing that children as young as five or six outwitted Nazi guards on a daily basis, that Jewish policemen helped the Germans control the ghetto, that children attended secret schools in the ghetto and even earned diplomas—these are the things that reveal the fabric of life, that can inspire, intrigue, and amaze.

Books in The Way People Live series allow both the casual reader and the student to see humans as victims, heroes, and onlookers. And although humans act in ways that can fill us with feelings of sorrow and revulsion, it is important to remember that "hero," "predator," and "victim" are dangerous terms. Heaping undue pity or praise on people reduces them to objects, and strips them of their humanity.

Seeing the Jews of Warsaw only as victims is to deny their humanity. Seeing them only as they appear in surviving photos, staring at the camera with infinite sadness, is limiting, both to them and to those who want to understand them. To an object of pity, the only appropriate response becomes "Those poor creatures!" and that reduces both the quality of their struggle and the depth of their despair. No one is served by such two-dimensional views of people and their cultures.

With this in mind, The Way People Live series strives to flesh out the traditional, two-dimensional views of people in various cultures and historical circumstances. Using a wide variety of primary quotations—the words not only of the politicians and government leaders, but of the real people whose lives are being examined—each book in the series attempts to show an honest and complete picture of a culture removed from our own by time or space.

By examining cultures in this way, the reader will notice not only the glaring differences from his or her own culture, but also will be struck by the similarities. For indeed, people share common needs—warmth, good company, stability, and affirmation from others. Ultimately, seeing how people really live, or have lived, can only enrich our understanding of ourselves.

"He Alone Who Owns the Youth Gains the Future"

In 1919 Adolf Hitler joined the German Workers' Party. In 1921 he assumed leadership of this party and renamed it the National Socialist German Workers' Party. In German, the party was called the *Nationalsozialistische Deutsche Arbeiterpartei*, and its members were called Nazis. The head of this party, Hitler, was called the führer—the German word for "leader."

Throughout the later part of the 1920s, the party became increasingly popular in Germany. Germany's government was a republic, much like the United States today, and parties campaigned to get their candidates elected to the Reichstag—the German congress—and also to the positions of president and chancellor. In the early 1930s the Nazi Party was the largest in the country. As a result of this popularity, Hitler was elected chancellor of Germany in 1933.

Three months after his election, Hitler and the Nazis succeeded in passing legislation in the Reichstag that gave Hitler absolute power to make all decisions for the country. This changed Germany's government from a republic to a dictatorship, a form of government in which one leader makes all of the decisions. Hitler was now the dictator of Germany and remained in this position until his death in 1945. This period in German history—while Hitler and the Nazis were in power, between 1933 and 1945—is often referred to as the Third Reich. It was during this time that Germany battled in World War II and the Holocaust occurred.

As a result of the power and popularity of the Nazi Party, Adolf Hitler was elected chancellor of Germany in 1933.

Hitler's dictatorship signaled a new period in German history. The Nazis began what is known as the *Gleichschaltung* ("coordination") of German society. Basically, the Nazis did not want any competition. They would not tolerate any opposition to their party and were intent on controlling every important aspect of German life from the army to education. Every facet of society was to be coordinated so that its actions and deeds fit with the National Socialist worldview. People who opposed the Nazis were to be removed from their posts and replaced by loyal party members. This way, the Nazis reasoned, the Third Reich would work as one large unit with a definite leader.

The Hitler Youth

In 1933 one aspect of German life that the National Socialists wished to control was youth life. With the Nazi rise to power, the Hitler Youth became the official state youth organization. Its goal was to bring as many eligible boys and girls as possible under its control. It took part in the *Gleichschaltung* and destroyed rival groups, bringing all youth groups in Germany under the power of the Hitler Youth. This process culminated in legislation in 1936 that made membership in the Hitler Youth mandatory for every eligible boy or girl between the ages of ten and eighteen and a follow-up decree in 1939 that meted

Members of the Hitler Youth salute their leader. Boys and girls between the ages of ten and eighteen were required by law to join the Hitler Youth.

out punishments for those who still refused to join. The Hitler Youth remained the official youth group of the German state for the twelve years that Hitler ruled Germany, and between 1939 and 1945 the term *Hitler Youth* was synonymous with *German Youth*.

Owning the Youth

On many occasions Hitler espoused the motto "He alone who owns the youth gains the future." The National Socialists wanted to utilize the Hitler Youth organization to do just that, "own" the German youth. At times they were able to accomplish this goal to an alarming degree. In the twelve years they were in power, the Nazis had unprecedented control over the lives of German children.

In an essay titled "Youth in the Third Reich," historian Detlev Peukert points out that during this time three different "generations" of Hitler Youth members passed through the group. The first of these were youngsters in their teens in 1933. These boys and girls lived their early, formative years in a democratic Germany before the Nazis came to power. The second generation of Hitler Youths were children who came of age between 1936 and 1939. These boys and girls had never known anything but a Germany with the National Socialists in power. Their schools and compulsory Hitler Youth membership had taught them Nazi ideology, and they knew no alternatives. The final generation of youngsters were those who came of age between 1939 and 1945. Like their predecessors, they knew no alternative to the Nazis. However, they were also adolescents in the years that Germany was engaged in World War II. The National Socialists controlled the lives of this generation more than any previous one.

This book focuses primarily on those boys and girls who spent their lives in the Hitler Youth. The Nazis influenced every aspect of the lives of boys and girls who entered their teenage years from 1936 to 1945. They influenced everything from the schools that boys and girls attended to the friends they chose and whom they dated. In nearly every way, the Nazis were able to "own" these youths.

Joining the Hitler Youth

"Swift as a greyhound, tough as leather, and hard as Krupp steel." This was the motto of every young German in the Hitler Youth, an organization designed to make young people physically fit, build their character, and train them in National Socialist ideology. When the Nazis came to power in 1933, it was their goal to persuade every qualified German boy and girl to be part of this organization. By 1940 the Hitler Youth had achieved this goal. But even though all qualified young Germans became members, it would be a mistake to assume that joining the Hitler Youth was a similar experience for all youngsters. Although the standards for qualification were the same for all, the divisions that children joined, their reasons for doing so, and even uniforms differed for each individual.

The Hitler Youth Formations

For most young Germans, involvement with the Hitler Youth began between the ages of four and six. At this time they entered grade school, where they were taught about National Socialism and the importance of joining the Hitler Youth. Then, at age ten, boys and girls became eligible for membership in the organization that they had heard so much about during their elementary years. Which Hitler Youth group a child joined depended on his or her age, gender, and performance. Each boy belonged to a unit of approximately fifteen members in one of seven formations,

or divisions (these seven divisions lasted the duration of World War II, whereas many other formations were founded and dissolved in a matter of months or years). Each girl's unit also had roughly fifteen members, but girls had only three formations. The uniform and activities of Hitler Youth members varied somewhat depending on the formation to which they were inducted. The Jungvolk was a Hitler Youth group for boys between the ages of ten and fourteen. Each one of its members—called *Pimpf*, meaning "Little Fellows"—received a performance book (*Leitungsbuch*). In these books, records were kept about each boy's growth, weight, speed, strength, military abilities—such as shooting, spying, and marching—and ideological growth (for instance, scores on tests of knowledge about Hitler and the National Socialists). Every entry had to be initialed by the boy's group leader to be considered official.

At age fourteen, boys left the Jungvolk and became eligible for promotion to the Hitlerjungend, or HJ, the Hitler Youth group that they would belong to until age eighteen. The performance book of each *Pimpf* was checked when he turned fourteen, and based on his accomplishments in the Jungvolk, he was either promoted to the HJ or was not allowed to advance. If promoted, there were many choices for new HJ members. Most Jungvolk joined the General (Allgemeine) HJ. However, boys who had performed well in the Jungvolk could apply for membership in elite formations of the group. Boys were

A Hitler Youth formation stands at attention. At age fourteen, boys left the Jungvolk and were eligible for promotion to the HJ.

selected for these divisions based not only on their performance in the Jungvolk, but also on their physical fitness, commitment to the cause of National Socialism, and educational accomplishments.

The most popular of these elite formations was the Air HJ. In this division, members received special airtraining that included learning about aviation through building and flying one-seat gliders. Alfons "Alfie" Heck, a former Air HJ member, recalls his first glider flight as an Air HJ member:

I was strapped down on the wooden seat of the basic glider SG 38, which was nothing more than an open laminated plywood beam with wings. . . . Twenty of my comrades grabbed a thick rubber rope and catapulted me into the air like the stone in a giant sling shot. The grass rushed at me, I pulled back on the stick and was airborne![1]

Boys who successfully completed a variety of glider test flights received their wings Classes A, B, and C. Members of the HJ lived at home, but they attended two- or three-week training courses at German air force, or Luftwaffe, bases. This was the most exciting aspect for many Air HJ members since they could see Luftwaffe pilots who frequently took them flying, allowing them to copilot bombers and fighters. In the early years of the Third Reich, participants in the Air HJ were then fed into the Air SA, a division of the Nazi Party. However, as war broke out and the need for manpower increased, Air HJ members were drafted directly into the Luftwaffe for military service.

Other HJ formations were similarly connected with party and military branches. The Motor HJ worked closely with the motorized divisions of the German army. Members of this division were taught to drive as well as the basics of mechanics for both domestic and foreign engines. The Naval HJ taught boys to sail. Here, they could obtain all of the necessary sailing certificates to enter German naval training. A Hitler Youth secret-police force, or *Streifendienst*, was created to infiltrate opposing groups and also reported any disobedient activities within the Hitler Youth. Members were chosen from the HJ and wore a blue-black stripe that read *"HJ-Streifendienst"* in yellow on their lower left arm. In a sense, members of this formation acted as

spies and were similar to the gestapo, the police in the Nazi state. Finally, in the Equestrian HJ, boys could learn about riding and caring for horses in preparation for joining the cavalry.

Not as many choices existed for young German girls, who belonged to one of three Hitler Youth formations. The National Socialists believed that the role of women in German society was to have genetically and racially healthy children. Therefore, the Hitler Youth organization strove to educate and prepare girls physically to be good, healthy mothers of the future soldiers of the German race. Between the ages of ten and fourteen, girls joined the Jungmädel, in which they began this education. Once a girl reached age fourteen, she was promoted into the League of German Girls, or Bund deutscher Mädel (BdM), and at age eighteen, she could become part of Faith and Beauty, a group for girls eighteen to twenty-one. The Hitler Youth did not offer any specialized or elite formations for girls.

A member of the Air HJ describes the features of a model glider to a group of Pimpfs. Boys in this formation also built and learned to fly full-sized gliders.

Qualifying for Membership

Not every German adolescent was allowed to become a member of the Hitler Youth. Each boy or girl had to meet four standards to join. The first of these standards was racial purity. Potential members could not have any Jewish ancestors. In the early days of Nazi Germany, some young Jewish Germans were excited about National Socialism and attempted to change this situation so that they might be part of the movement. However, their requests were not heard and all Jewish youth were denied membership. Any boy or girl with a Jewish ancestor was also denied entry, as were children with ancestors from other races that the Nazis believed were inferior. This included anyone of African, Chinese, Polish, or Indian descent, and basically all people of color. (The Japanese were an exception, as they were Germany's World War II ally. In fact, Japanese youth groups were included in a variety of international Hitler Youth rallies.)

Once potential members were determined to be racially pure by Nazi standards, they then had to prove that no hereditary diseases ran in their family. Hereditary diseases are diseases passed from parent to child through genes. In Nazi Germany, the following conditions were defined as hereditary diseases: "epilepsy, schizophrenia (as evidenced by moodiness or temper tantrums, indifferent housekeeping in women or irregular employment patterns in men), deafness, dumbness, prostitution, mental retardation, and certain forms of venereal disease."[2] Alcoholics, homosexuals, and people with birth defects, and hemophilia were also included in this category. It is important to realize that this list would be considered incorrect by today's scientific standards. Since the end of World War II, scientists have discovered that many of the "diseases" included here are neither dis-

eases—for example, homosexuality and prostitution—nor are they hereditary—for example, venereal diseases. Also, "indifferent housekeeping" would no longer be considered a symptom of schizophrenia. In the case of the Hitler Youth, however, any candidate having one of these "diseases" was automatically ineligible to join. If a parent or sibling was afflicted with one of these diseases, then it was up to the Hitler Youth organization to determine whether the candidate could join.

Once the ancestry and hereditary fitness of a boy or girl satisfied Nazi standards, the Hitler Youth organization made certain that the child had no "objectionable" political attitudes. This

Girls of the BdM prepare breakfast while camping in the countryside. This Hitler Youth branch strove to teach girls the skills they would need to be good mothers.

meant that children who behaved poorly during their trial membership period might not be accepted. It also meant that former members of Communist or Socialist groups had difficulty joining the organization. In reality, this was not such a problem since many young people who were aligned with the Communists and Socialists were creating a "united front of working youth for the struggle against the Hitler dictatorship"[3] and did not desire to be in the Hitler Youth. This standard did pose a problem, however, for young people whose parents had been associated with these movements. Even if these children wanted to be members, some were not allowed to join. Finally, once youngsters met all of these standards, they had one more thing to prove—that they were physically fit or could quickly become fit. Many boys and girls with conditions such as asthma had difficulty meeting this requirement and were therefore not allowed to join.

Deciding to Join

Standards for admission were strict, but the National Socialists were insistent that every child who qualified should join the Hitler Youth. Therefore, although some boys and girls joined out of commitment to National Socialism, others were drawn to the group because of measures taken by the organization to encourage and force membership. This created a unique atmosphere in Hitler Youth groups where ardent Nazis marched alongside those who disliked Nazism, and those who loved being in the group participated with youngsters who hated it. Most boys and girls probably joined for a combination of reasons—not just one.

The first, perhaps most obvious reason for becoming a member of the Hitler Youth was a genuine belief in National Socialism and its goals. William Allen, a former member, says he joined "simply because I wanted to be in a boys' club where I could strive towards the nationalistic ideal."[4] Baldur von Schirach, the head of the Hitler Youth, assured boys and girls that his organization was the best place for them. He guaranteed that "he who marches in the Hitler Youth is not a number among millions, but an individual soldier of an idea. . . . The best Hitler Youth is the one who . . . identifies completely with the National Socialist ideology."[5]

Whereas some young people probably did understand and identify with the philosophy of Nazism, others may have joined the Hitler Youth to do something meaningful with their lives. The words and actions of Hitler and the National Socialists made it very clear that young Germans could play a meaningful role in the improvement of Germany by joining the group. One former member testifies to this sense of purpose:

> When I raised three fingers of my right hand to the sky in the oath to the *Führer*, my left gripping the flag of my unit, my spine tingled in the conviction that I now belonged to something both majestic and threatened by bitter enemies. It was *Deutschland* (Germany).[6]

Hitler frequently told boys and girls that Germany's future was in their hands. It was their destiny to "be guarantors for the security of the existence and thus the future of [the] German people."[7] In response, some young people sought membership to fulfill what they believed to be a noble goal or, as a BdM member put it, to "break out from [their] childish, narrow [lives] and attach it to something that was great and essential."[8]

Hitler was not just paying lip service to the importance of young people, he backed up his

The Law Concerning the Hitler Youth

In order to achieve the National Socialist goal of having every eligible young German in the Hitler Youth, it became necessary for Baldur von Schirach to write and pass the Law Concerning the Hitler Youth. The law, reprinted below, was passed on December 1, 1936. It not only made membership in the Hitler Youth mandatory, it also gave Schirach a promotion to "Youth Leader of the German Reich." Now, Schirach reported directly to Hitler, showing how important the Hitler Youth was to Hitler and the Nazis. The document was taken from Peter D. Stachura's book *The German Youth Movement, 1900–1945: An Interpretative and Documentary History.*

"The Law for the Hitler Youth, 1 December 1936:

The future of the German nation depends on its youth. The whole of German youth must therefore be prepared for its future duties. The Reich Government has accordingly decided on the following law, which is published herewith:

1. The whole of German youth within the frontiers of the Reich is organized in the Hitler Youth.

2. The whole of German youth is to be educated, outside the parental home and school, in the Hitler Youth physically, intellectually and morally in the spirit of Na-

tional Socialism for service to the nation and community.

3. The task of educating the whole of German youth in the Hitler Youth is being entrusted to the Reich Youth Leader of the NSDAP (National Socialists). He is therefore 'Youth Leader of the German Reich.' He has the status of a Supreme Reich Authority with headquarters in Berlin and he is directly responsible to the *Führer* and Reich Chancellor.

4. The requisite legal decrees and general administrative orders for the carrying out and supplementation of the Law will be issued by the *Führer* and Reich Chancellor.

Berlin, 1 December 1936

The *Führer* and Reich Chancellor
　　Adolf Hitler"

Baldur von Schirach, the head of the Hitler Youth from 1931–1940.

words with his actions. The National Socialists allowed youth to have a great deal of power and influence in their movement. The organization was built on the idea of "youth leading youth" and offered powerful leadership positions for boys and girls. Also, children who were members of the Hitler Youth received a

variety of special privileges. They were considered an elite group in the same way that the SA (the adult Nazi Party members called storm troopers) and the SS (an elite guard of party members; only the most racially pure individuals could be SS members) were. This meant that they were allowed to march alongside these groups during party rallies and parades. The Hitler Youth secret police also assisted in inquiries, guard duty, investigations, and finding missing persons. In today's United States, this would be roughly equivalent to the Boy Scouts aiding in military police investigations.

The power they could have and the active role they could play in the National Socialist movement probably attracted many young Germans to the Hitler Youth. But perhaps most importantly, Hitler himself spoke to the group, met with youth leaders, and decorated young boys and girls for their service to Germany. One Hitler Youth recalls that when "the *Führer* beamed down on us, his eyes caught mine—I was absolutely sure of that, as was every one of my comrades."[9] Indeed, actually meeting and seeing the führer made quite an impression on many Hitler Youth members. After all, the supreme leader of their country was listening to them.

Although the feeling of importance the Nazis instilled in boys and girls and the desire to strive for the National Socialist ideal were common reasons for joining, it is not surprising that some boys and girls also joined to rebel against their parents. A BdM member remembers one reason she joined was "because it strengthened [her] opposition against [her] conservative home."[10] The Hitler Youth did indeed "strengthen" this position because in many ways it had more power than a child's parents.

Some parents did not want their children to join. In some circles, the Jungvolk and HJ were seen as groups of rowdy boys with too little supervision, and BdM members had a reputation for being sexually promiscuous. This opinion was reinforced by propaganda—information that is carefully presented and spread to promote a cause—that encouraged BdM girls to have babies for the führer at a young age and by the high number of pregnant girls within the BdM ranks.

However, parents had little control over whether their children joined and actually very little control in general. The Nazis encouraged young people's first loyalty be to the National Socialist state instead of to their families. Baldur von Schirach told parents that "the lives of all German youths belong solely to Hitler."[11] Interference with a child's desire to join or even openly disagreeing with Nazi ideology in front

Bearing flags, a Hitler Youth group passes by a formation of troops. The Hitler Youth also marched alongside SA and SS members during rallies and parades.

of a son or daughter could result in serious consequences for parents. Hitler warned that if they did not change their minds and believe in Nazism, "then [the Nazis] will take the children away from them."[12] It soon became illegal to prohibit a child from joining. Thus, if a child went against his or her parents' wishes, the parents were the ones who were in trouble with the government—not the children. In this way, the Nazis undermined parents who did not want their children to join the group. Young

people knew their parents had no control over their membership, and some members may have joined solely to defy their parents.

Encouraged to Join

Although some adolescents joined purely out of choice, the Nazis also took measures to encourage membership in the Hitler Youth. Hitler's seeming commitment to the power

Hitler Youth Meets Hitler

In his book *The Burden of Hitler's Legacy*, Alfons Heck discusses how he felt in 1944 when Hitler personally decorated him with a medal for his work in the Hitler Youth.

"[The man] literally made my knees shake. I had seen him on four previous occasions, but never in an intimate setting face to face. The man was Adolf Hitler.

The *Führer* wore his usual wartime attire: field gray tunic over black trousers with a white shirt and tie, no belt, no hat. The Iron Cross I Class on his breast pocket was his only decoration; he earned it in World War I as a corporal and wore it on all his uniforms. . . .

The unexpectedness of his appearance was awesome. . . . We greeted him with a thunderous 'Heil, mein Führer (Salute my Führer)!'

He told us briefly that very soon the tide of the war would turn in our favor . . . Hitler's power of persuasion was magical. 'We shall launch an all-out offensive which will not only deny our enemies the holy soil of Germany, but will throw them back into the sea,' asserted the *Führer*. 'Then we will take care of the [Russians] in short shrift.'. . . It seemed like a tall

order, but I had no doubt we would succeed. . . .

Months of gnawing fear culminated in surging elation when we filed past Hitler on our way out. Not only was I meeting the man who held our destiny in his hands . . . but he greeted me with fatherly kindness as I came to attention before him. 'I know I can depend on you to do your duty to the end,' [Hitler said].

'Jawohl, mein Führer (Of course, my Führer),' I whispered, hoarse with emotion. I returned the slightest pressure of his moist hand and stared into his surprisingly light-blue eyes. As if in a time suspension, I was aware of every feature in his pale face. His cheeks were blotched from the exertion of his speech and there was a razor nick in the corner of his upper lip. To the fraction of an inch, he was as tall as I, five feet eight inches. . . . The colonel, a hero with the Knights Cross around his neck, handed him a velvet case with the War Service Cross I. Class with Swords. Hitler didn't pin it on my chest, but passed it to me with a slightly trembling hand.

'Danke, mein Führer (Thank you, my Führer),' I saluted, repressing a tear of emotion, and he lifted his hand. I was dismissed."

Kommende

Sporting events such as this variation of a Roman chariot race were used to encourage boys to join the Hitler Youth.

and respect of young people did make some boys and girls desire to commit themselves to him personally. However, the Nazis also recognized the potential to use this desire and created an advertising campaign to encourage boys and girls to join the Hitler Youth. Young Germans were told that they could make Hitler happy and give him a wonderful gift by joining the group for the führer's next birth-

day. Existing Hitler Youth groups launched recruitment campaigns that included parades, marches, and events such as choir concerts in hopes that they could bolster membership.

The Hitler Youth also encouraged membership by offering many fun and exciting activities. A former member recalls that he and his friends "could hardly wait to join the Hitler Youth. [They] craved action, which was offered

In uniform, Hitler Youths study for their school exams. Members often wore their uniforms all day.

in abundance. There was the monotonous drill, but that could be endured for the opportunity to hike, camp, enact war games in the field and play a variety of sports."[13] Being persuaded by friends—peer pressure—was most likely a common reason for becoming part of the group. In fact, once the Nazis came to power in 1933, joining became fashionable, so many young people did just that.

The National Socialists also enticed many boys and girls to join by offering a chance to get out of school and homework. Hitler Youth activities often interfered with school. Teachers had to let members go and were forbidden to assign them makeup work or homework of any kind. Those boys and girls who were not members were left in the classroom to study and do homework while their Hitler Youth friends played exciting games outside of school. This may have drawn many to join the group.

Finally, the Nazis tried to attract young people to their organization by creating elaborate uniforms and accessories for Hitler Youth formations. Many young boys were excited to receive their knives with a swastika on the handle. Hitler himself placed a great deal of emphasis on uniforms in his speeches to young people. He stressed that their "uniform shall be for you a perpetual reminder of . . . the unity of the German people."[14] The uniforms differed according to age and gender, but all conveyed a sense of membership, unity, and dignity.

Being Coerced into Joining

Even with all of these reasons to join, many young people still did not seek membership in the Hitler Youth. Since the goal of the National Socialists was to have every German youth who qualified become a member, the organization took measures to make certain that the lives of young people who refused membership would be more difficult. One of the first things that National Socialists did to accomplish this was to eliminate all other alternatives. As part of the *Gleichschaltung,* they banned all competing youth groups, including sports and church groups. As a result, young people who wanted to be part of a club had no choice but to join the Hitler Youth.

Ostracism (the act of excluding a person from a group) was an important tool used by the National Socialists to coerce German boys and girls into joining the Hitler Youth. Schirach explained that the Nazis counted on this, knowing that "youngsters who did not join the Hitler Youth were at a disadvantage in that they could not take part in our camping, in our trips, in our sporting meets. They were in a certain sense outsiders of the youth life." [15] For instance, since Hitler Youth activities often started immediately after school, leaving no time to go home and change, members frequently wore their uniforms all day. Those who were not wearing uniforms at school were obviously not members of the Hitler Youth and were therefore social outcasts. The fear of being an outcast and the desire to fit in by wearing the same clothes as other classmates may have drawn some youngsters to the group.

Although uniforms were one way of making nonmembers feel as though they were "outsiders," this was a relatively mild form of ostracism. Young people also faced more severe consequences if they did not join. The Nazis were able to make school life very difficult for nonmembers. The Hitler Youth taught its members that "he who is not prepared to bear [Hitler's] name will therefore not be regarded as a friend of National Socialism." [16] Nonmembers were defined as enemies of the state and were teased and harassed by their peers—at times, even by their former friends. Teachers also teased and harassed nonmembers at school. In order to

be a teacher in Nazi Germany, educators had to be party members or at least had to join the National Socialist Teachers' League. Some of these teachers willingly exerted pressure on students to join the Hitler Youth, some were offered incentives, and still others were forced to promote the group in order to keep their jobs. To pressure students into joining, teachers sometimes gave nonmembers difficult homework that was not assigned to their Hitler Youth counterparts, and some teachers even physically threatened and harassed them. In a 1934 letter, a Catholic priest complained about such occurrences:

> Last Saturday [the teacher assigned] those boys [not in the Hitler Youth] the essay: "Why I am not in the Hitler Youth?", while all the other children in class had no homework. On [assigning] the essay he added: "If you don't write the essay I shall beat you until you can't sit down.". . . The teacher's pressure on the [Catholic] Youth Club members even goes so far as to threaten the boys that he would "muck up" their reports at Easter and would not move them up, and so on. [17]

Some nonmembers may have chosen to join rather than endure this type of punishment from their classmates and teachers.

However, being teased, beaten, and having more homework were not the only problems faced by individuals refusing to join the Hitler Youth. The National Socialists took other measures to make life difficult. They made Hitler Youth membership necessary to obtain a variety of jobs in Nazi Germany. If a young person was not a member of the Hitler Youth, then he or she could not be a teacher, a civil servant, or enter a variety of other professions. The Nazis also refused to promote parents whose children were not members.

Some young Germans may have joined in order to have future career options or merely to make certain that their parents had opportunities to advance. Also, the fact that membership was required for future work meant that some parents probably encouraged and/or pressured their children to join to keep both their own and their child's options open.

In 1936, after three years of being in power in Germany, and in spite of all of their recruiting, some qualified boys and girls were still not members of the Hitler Youth. To achieve their goal of total youth membership, the Nazis passed the "Law Concerning the Hitler Youth" on December 1, 1936. The decree made membership in the Hitler Youth mandatory: Every qualified boy or girl over the age of ten was required to join. As a result of this law, 2.5 million more young people joined and 97 percent of German boys and girls were members by 1939. To recruit the last 3 percent, a second law was passed in 1939 that gave orders as to how the 1936 decree would be enforced. It made the Hitler Youth a compulsory service, much like a military draft. At that point, all young Germans of "pure blood" had to join the Hitler Youth or suffer very real consequences.

The Initiation Ceremony

Once German boys and girls met all of the standards for joining the Hitler Youth and decided or were forced to do so, they participated in an initiation ceremony in which they swore an oath to Hitler and the Hitler Youth. This was an important occasion for many girls and boys. The ceremony was typically done on April 20—Hitler's birthday—and it was usually held in a big hall or castle decorated with torches, candles, and banners. In this solemn atmosphere, an important party official would make a speech reminding the boys or girls about the significance of the day and their role in National Socialism. After the speaker was done, the young people took an oath: "I promise in the Hitler Youth to do my duty at all times in love and faithfulness to help the Führer—so help me God."[18] The oath differed slightly for girls and included a sentence about self-sacrifice. But once the oath at a given ceremony was completed, a military band burst into patriotic songs with trumpets blaring. The new Hitler Youths were now trial members. This trial period would last from two to six months. During this time the racial and hereditary background of the boy or girl would be checked as well as their commitment to Germany. In his book *The Hitler Youth*, H. W. Koch explains what happened at the end of this trial period for a *Pimpf:*

> This period was concluded by a special test, combining sport, close combat, and questions of an "ideological" nature (mainly on the history of the National Socialist Party), culminating in a *Mütprobe*, a courage test which could take the form of having to jump in full battle-dress and boots from the window of the first floor of a block of flats [apartments].[19]

If the boy passed these tests, he was then an official member of the Jungvolk and on his way to the HJ. However, if he failed to pass the test, he was made to feel as though his life was at an end and he would be better off dead. Failure meant he was a social outcast, physically unfit to be a part of Germany.

The Uniform

Each initiated Hitler Youth received a uniform. These uniforms differed according to which formation the young person joined.

When young people were admitted into a branch of the Hitler Youth, there was always an elaborate ceremony. The following is a guide for youth leaders to use to create this ceremony, including the speech that should be made. It is reprinted from Jeremy Noakes and Geoffrey Pridham's *Documents on Nazism, 1919–1945*.

"Ceremony of admission into the Cubs of the German *Jungvolk*

It is of the greatest importance that the admissions are arranged in a solemn way. For everybody the hour of his induction must be a great experience. The cub [*Pimpf*] and young lass must regard this hour of their first vow to the Führer as the holiest of their whole life.

Text of the speech of the Jungvolk leader, to be read in all branches:
Dear boy!/Dear girl!

This hour in which you are to be received into the great community of the Hitler Youth is a very happy one and at the same time will introduce you into a new period of your lives. Today for the first time you swear allegiance to the Führer which will bind you to him for all time.

And every one of you, my young comrades, enters at this moment into the community of all German boys and girls. With your vow and your commitment you now become a bearer of German spirit and German honour. Every one, every single one, now becomes the foundation for an eternal Reich of all Germans.

When you too now march in step with the youngest soldiers, then bear in mind that this march is to train you to be a National Socialist conscious of the future and faithful to his duty.

And the Führer demands of you and of us all that we train ourselves to a life of service and duty, of loyalty and comradeship. You, ten-year-old cubs, and you lasses are not too young nor too small to practise obedience and discipline, to integrate yourself into the community and show yourself to be a comrade. Like you, millions of young Germans are today swearing allegiance to the Führer and here, before your parents, the Party and your comrades, we now receive you into our great community of loyalty. Your motto will always be:

'Führer, command—we follow!'

(*The cubs are asked to rise.*) Now, say after me: 'I promise always to do my duty in the Hitler Youth in love and loyalty to the Führer and to our flag.'"

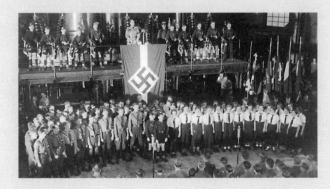

Elaborate ceremonies such as this one were held to initiate boys and girls into the Hitler Youth.

The Response of a *Pimpf*

For members of the Jungvolk, being denied promotion to the HJ was a terrible fate. In *Education for Death*, Gregor Ziemer tells the story of the drastic reaction of one *Pimpf* to not being promoted.

"How seriously the *Pimpf* takes his rank I realized when I talked to Hermann P., a broken-hearted German father whose boy had been refused permission to attend the graduation exercises of his troop. His *Leistungsbuch* showed excellent marks; he had fulfilled all the rigid requirements. But he had been told quite openly that he could not be promoted because his father was not as good a Nazi as he should be!

The boy knew what that meant. If he was not promoted to the *Jungvolk*, he could never become a Hitler Youth. No Hitler Youth, no S.A. No S.A., no position, no job, no rank, nothing.

'I found him a few nights ago on the kitchen floor unconscious,' the father told me. 'While his mother and I were attending an anti-air-raid rehearsal, he stuffed newspapers under the door and turned on the gas. We barely saved his life. I have now signed a paper that I will join the *Arbeitsfront*, and become active in the party. After all—my life is lived. I was in the last war, and all that. But the boy—he must have his chance. He took the signed paper to his *Gruppenleiter* (group leader). They are going to promote him now.'"

The basic uniform for boys resembled those of the SA. Boys wore heavy black shoes with short black stockings, black shorts, a brown shirt with a swastika armband, and a trench cap. As they moved through the Hitler Youth ranks, they gathered uniform accessories. For example, when the *Pimpf* was officially inducted into the Jungvolk, he received Jungvolk insignias to put on his brown shirt and a shoulder strap. He was also given two knives: a scout knife and a knife in the shape of the bayonet of the German army.

The HJ had several different uniforms. The General HJ kept the same uniform as the Jungvolk and added HJ insignias. However, the Air HJ wore uniforms similar to those of the Luftwaffe. They were Luftwaffe blue, with light blue piping, and they included the armband of the HJ. Just as the Air HJ wore uniforms similar to those of the Luftwaffe, the uniforms of the Motor, Naval, and Equestrian HJ formations resembled those of the army, navy, and cavalry, respectively.

The girls' uniforms "called *Kluften*, include[d] heavy marching shoes, stockings . . . full blue skirts, white blouses, cotton neckerchiefs with wooden rings bearing the group insignia. For bad weather the girls [had] heavy blue 'training suits,' slacks, and capes."[20] They, too, went through an initiation ceremony and swore an oath to Hitler before receiving their insignias. When they were promoted to the BdM, their basic uniform remained the same but looked much more elaborate, covered in BdM "emblems, letters, triangles and swastikas."[21] Once boys and girls were outfitted in these new uniforms and initiated into their Hitler Youth divisions, they were considered official members of the Hitler Youth.

The Race War

It is impossible to understand the life of Hitler Youth members without first understanding the unique way that they were taught to view the world. One of the primary objectives of the organization was to teach young boys and girls about National Socialist weltanschauung, meaning "worldview" or "ideology." The foundation of this ideology was a combination of social Darwinism and eugenics that culminated in a conviction that humankind was engaged in a race war. Every other aspect of the National Socialist worldview originated from this belief.

Evolution and Social Darwinism

Douglas J. Futuyma, an evolutionary biologist, points out that "in the broadest sense, evolution is merely change, and so is all-pervasive; galaxies, languages, and political systems all evolve."[22] Biological evolution "is a process that results in heritable (hereditary) changes in a population spread over many generations."[23] In 1859 Charles Darwin published *The Origins of Species*, in which he explained his theory of biological evolution. According to Darwin's theory, hereditary changes over many generations were caused by three different factors: variation, natural selection, and the struggle for survival of the fittest.

For example, in a forest, the green caterpillars with red spots live on the green leaves of the trees, eating and reproducing. Their green color matches the leaves and makes it difficult for the birds to find and eat them. Every year, new caterpillars are born, and then one year three caterpillars with no spots are born. Darwin would call the fact that some caterpillars are born without spots variation. This means that organisms spontaneously change from one generation to the next. The green caterpillars are even more difficult for the birds to see because they have no red spots and blend into the leaves. As a result, they live longer and have more offspring, some of

The Nazis taught the Hitler Youth that Charles Darwin's theory of biological evolution could be applied to societies.

which also have no spots. The offspring with no spots also live longer and have more offspring than their spotted counterparts. This goes on for many generations until most of the caterpillars born have no spots.

Thus if the result of variation is favorable to a species—meaning it helps the organism live longer—then the individual organism will be more likely to reproduce. Some of its offspring will inherit this new trait. These youngsters will then live longer and reproduce themselves. In comparison, if a yellow caterpillar were born, it would be more easily seen by birds and would be eaten. Yellow caterpillars would be *less* likely to live long enough to produce offspring. Therefore, yellow is not a favorable trait. This process, which results in

Francis Galton believed that humankind could accelerate its own evolution through eugenics.

the survival of only those organisms that have a favorable variation, is called natural selection.

The survival of the fittest is closely related to natural selection. It refers to the fact that in this process different variations of a species struggle for existence. The fittest variation—the variation that is hereditarily best fit to live in the environment (in this example, the variation of caterpillar that is best suited to live on a green leaf)—survives but other variations, the spotted or yellow caterpillars, die out. This survival of the fittest, in combination with variation and natural selection, made up the processes that Darwin thought explained biological evolution.

In the 1920s and 1930s, a variety of people began to apply Darwin's ideas to a new realm. They applied his theory of biological evolution to society. The result was a theory called social Darwinism. Social Darwinists believed that human beings were also engaged in the processes of natural selection and the struggle for the survival of the fittest. They believed that the struggle for survival of the fittest human beings created human progress such as scientific discoveries and wealth.

Eugenics

How could a people speed up their own process of evolution and human progress? Eugenics seemed to offer the answer. Eugenics came about in 1869 when Francis Galton, a cousin of Charles Darwin, wrote a book entitled *Hereditary Genius: An Inquiry into Its Laws and Consequences.* Galton thought humankind could accelerate its own evolution if it stopped relying on the haphazard process of natural selection. Therefore, eugenicists believed that they could control the reproduction of favorable and unfavorable traits by planning marriage and reproduction.

Hereditary Measures

The National Socialist belief in the race war, and the solutions that eugenics seemed to offer, prompted the Nazis to take legal measures in line with their eugenic beliefs. One such measure was the 1933 "Law for the Protection of Hereditary Health: The Attempt to Improve the German Aryan Breed." This law is excerpted from Louis L. Snyder's *Hitler's Third Reich: A Documentary History*.

"ARTICLE 1: (1.) Anyone who suffers from an inheritable disease may be sterilized surgically if, in the judgment of medical science, it could be expected that his descendants will suffer from serious inherited mental or physical defects.

(2.) Anyone who suffers from one of the following is to be regarded as inheritably diseased within the meaning of this law:
1. congenital feeble-mindedness
2. schizophrenia
3. manic-depression
4. congenital epilepsy
5. inheritable St. Vitus dance (Huntington's Chorea)
6. hereditary blindness
7. hereditary deafness
8. serious inheritable malformations

(3.) In addition, anyone suffering from chronic alcoholism may also be sterilized.

ARTICLE 2: (1.) Anyone who requests sterilization is entitled to it. If he be incapacitated or under a guardian because of his low state of mental health or not yet 18 years of age, his legal guardian is empowered to make the request. In other cases of limited capacity the request must receive the approval of the legal representative. If a person be of age and has a nurse, the latter's consent is required. . . .

ARTICLE 3: Sterilization may also be recommended by (1.) the official physician, (2.) the official in charge of a hospital, sanitarium, or prison."

There is a very important difference between Darwin's theories of biological evolution and the "science" of eugenics. Darwin believed that evolution could explain change that had already occurred. He never believed that he, or anyone else, could predict what traits were favorable and would be naturally selected in the future. However, this is exactly what Galton proposed—that evolutionary theory could be used to predict future evolution.

The goal of eugenicists was to "improve the breed" or to increase the population of "fit" human beings by carefully deciding who should have children with whom. As in the case of the social Darwinists, they believed the acceleration of evolution would cause an equal acceleration of human progress in culture, science, and technologies. Eugenicists decided that certain traits, such as intelligence, strength, and wealth, were favorable and told people who had these traits that they should mate with others of the same group. Most importantly, people in these marriages must have many children. This way, there would be more offspring from this "fit" group.

Eugenicists also called for the elimination of the "unfit," those they felt had unfavorable traits—the less intelligent, weaker, and poorer population and people with hereditary illnesses. They believed that these people should have fewer children or none at all; this way, the "unfit" population would decrease. Eugenicists argued that people having hereditary illnesses should not have any children.

At a rally, Hitler Youth perform their daily exercise routine. Eugenicists considered physical strength to be a favorable trait.

They reasoned that these illnesses or unfavorable traits would then disappear from the population more quickly. Humankind would not have to go through generations with these mutations being slowly eliminated; instead, it could be done in one generation. The next generation would then be free of these diseases, and the highly gifted race would be that much closer.

Life Is a Struggle

The theories of social Darwinism and eugenics were popular all over the world. Everywhere social Darwinist and eugenic organizations were founded with many excited new members. Adolf Hitler drew heavily on these ideas in the formation of his weltanschauung—a worldview that would eventually become the foundation of the ideology of National Socialism. This ideology was a hodgepodge of ideas pieced together that made little logical sense as a whole. It tended to focus on being in opposition to institutions and ideas, but it offered little to replace them once they were gone. It was this ideology that members of the Hitler Youth were taught to revere.

They learned that, first and foremost, life was a struggle for survival of the fittest. It was an individual struggle in which "he who wants to live should fight . . . and he who does not want to battle in this world of eternal struggle does not deserve to be alive."[24] This world was a cruel place where one must fight or die, and it was necessary for the strong to conquer the weak without compassion or pity. This idea is often referred to as "might is right" because whoever wins a fight is right since he or she had to be stronger (mightier) in order to win. It even justifies murder since the murderer is right to have killed his weaker victim. Therefore, the most important thing for a young Hitler Youth member was to be strong.

Hitler Youth members worked to become strong not only to assure their survival as individuals but also to secure the victory of their species, or variation of human being, over all others. Boys and girls were educated to believe that just as plants and animals could be divided into species, so too could human beings. These species, called races, were "made up of a group of people . . . distinguished from all other groups of people by a combination of endowed physical features and spiri-

tual characteristics and which repeatedly reproduced its own kind."[25] In other words, the National Socialists defined a race as a group of people who looked alike and who, they assumed, acted and thought alike as well.

The Hitler Youth were taught that race determined not only the physical characteristics of individual people but also their spiritual and mental characteristics. Genetic physical traits such as skull size and shape were thought to determine mental capabilities and personality traits. Basically, the National Socialists believed that what today would be called stereotypes were scientific facts. Groups of people were said to be hereditarily lazy, stupid, or evil. Being cautious or talking too much was considered an unfavorable hereditary variation in human beings, whereas being a hard worker was thought to be favorable.

Hitler Youth leaders taught that these races could be placed into three categories:

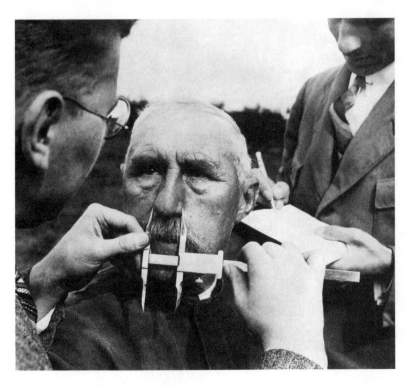

A man's nose is measured to determine his racial background. Other characteristics such as skull size and shape were used to determine mental capability.

culture founders, culture maintainers, and culture destroyers. Life, they said, was not only a struggle for the individual to exist, it was also a struggle between races that were the founders, maintainers, and destroyers of culture.

The Fit

The National Socialists maintained that they had figured out which races belonged in each of these three categories. They alleged to have gone back through history, studied all of the advances in civilization, and claimed to have used tests to determine the heredity of various

The idea that the Nordic race was made up of people who were tall, slender, and had rosy white skin and blond hair is illustrated in this poster of "The German Student."

historical societies and figures. The Nazis concluded that all significant advances had been made by the Nordic (Aryan) race and, therefore, this was the only race of culture founders. Hitler told his followers that "human culture today, the results of art, science, and techniques, [was] almost exclusively the creative product of the Aryan."[26] On this sketchy basis, the Nazis told boys and girls that the Nordic race was superior—the fittest.

It was said that the Nordic race was made up of people who were tall and slender, had a small face, a high-set nose, rosy white skin, smooth golden-blond hair, and light blue to gray eyes. *The Nazi Primer: Official Handbook for Schooling the Hitler Youth* listed the following as the Aryan's racial personality:

> It is uncommonly gifted mentally. It is outstanding for truthfulness and energy. Nordic men for the most part possess, even in regard to themselves, a great power of judgment. . . . They are persistent and stick to a purpose when once they have set themselves to it. Their energy is displayed not only in warfare but also in technology and in scientific research. They are predisposed to leadership by nature.[27]

The young members also learned that the Nordic race was the "principal ingredient" of the German people, making up 50 percent of the Germanic race (defined as the people living in Germany who were not foreign, Jewish, or a person of color.) According to the National Socialists, Germany was home to the world's largest population of Nordics; therefore, it was the "fittest" country, the one that should lead all others. In other words, the Hitler Youth were taught that they were members of the fittest race and citizens of the greatest country on earth.

In the February 1941 issue of *Survey Graphic*, Robert L. H. Hiller attempted to explain how the boys and girls of the Hitler Youth viewed the world. Hiller was a young U.S. citizen who, during his boyhood in Germany, had been "swept up" in the Hitler Youth movement. From this perspective, he attempts to explain how young Hitler Youths believe that might is right.

"This boy is one of the finest people I know. I have spent many nights with him, discussing literature, art, religion, every topic in which a college boy would be interested, and he has surprised me often with his sincerity, and sensitive understanding. But that day he told me that he had struck several people because they did not salute the [Nazi] flags. I am sure he had no realization of the injustice and the brutality of beating people who did not have the power to fight back. All he could see was that it was something he felt Germany demanded from him.

To them strength is the greatest virtue. That everything good is strong is one explanation of their racial creed. Since they are the bearers of righteousness, their race must be better. They do accept the existence of other races. But they make a distinction between good and bad races, and the bad ones are the ones that, in their eyes, are weak. It is easy to call the Jews weak, and therefore bad [because there were so few Jewish people in Germany compared to Aryans]. . . . It is easy, under these premises, to call any nation weak, and therefore bad, that stands in one's way."

The Hitler Youth and the Race War

The ultimate goal of the National Socialists and the German state was the preservation of this Nordic race. The Hitler Youth were told that "in this world human culture and civilization [were] inseparably bound up with the existence of the Aryan. His dying-off or his decline would again lower upon the earth the dark veils of a time without culture."[28] To keep culture alive, the Hitler Youth organization told its members that they must work to purify the Aryan race and fight against their racial enemies, the culture destroyers—who, according to the Nazis, were the Jewish people. This racial battle between culture founders and culture destroyers was called a race war.

The Hitler Youth played an important role in the race war in Germany. Although troops fought at the front beginning in 1939, the race war began earlier and took place all over Germany. The very existence of the Hitler Youth helped in this war since the qualifications for membership in the organization required that boys and girls be "racially pure." The boys and girls who were eligible were those considered of good blood, and those who were not members were seen as undesirables. In this way, the organization helped separate those whom the Nazis deemed "fit" from the "unfit."

This was not the only reason why the Hitler Youth was a valuable tool for the Nazis in the race war, though. It also helped the Nazis attain some of their positive eugenic goals. Positive eugenics are measures that

Two American soldiers examine the burned remains of an inmate at Dachau. Some members of the Hitler Youth were shocked when they were shown evidence of the Holocaust.

encourage reproduction of "fit" populations. The National Socialists believed this fit population was the Aryan population. Their first goal was to purify the Aryan race, and achieving this began with youngsters tending to their own personal racial health as representatives of this race. This was done by increasing physical fitness through athletic sporting activities.

Members were also told to remain "racially pure" over the course of their lives. They learned that the two threats to this racial purity were blood-mixing and hereditary illness. Blood-mixing was defined as two people from different races having sex and/or children. The Nazis believed that if a human being of the superior race had a child with someone inferior, the result would be a child that was racially in between the two parents—not as superior as the Aryan parent. The other threat to the German bloodline, according to the National Socialists, was hereditary illness.

The Nazis argued that Hitler Youths should not mate with people having these illnesses. This way, they believed, no hereditary illness would occur in the next generation of Aryans. A member could remain pure by avoiding blood-mixing and hereditary illness his or her entire life.

Another measure Nazis wanted to achieve through the Hitler Youth was encouraging female members to have many children to increase the Aryan population. From early childhood, members of the Jungmädel were taught that men fought the military wars and women were responsible for part of the race war. Hitler told women that

the sacrifices which the man makes in the struggle of his nation, the woman makes in the preservation of that nation in individual cases. What the man gives in courage on the battlefield, the woman gives in eternal self-sacrifice, in eternal pain and suffering. Every child that a woman brings into the world is a battle, a battle waged for the existence of her people.[29]

The BdM encouraged girls to carefully choose a healthy Aryan mate at a young age and have many children. The Nazis also encouraged young girls to have illegitimate children. Propaganda told young women that it was better to have a child out of wedlock than not at all. The National Socialists praised the "heroic 'racially pure' unmarried mother's loyalty to the Führer."[30] By encouraging "pure," strong, and healthy Aryan couples to have many children, the Hitler Youth aided the eugenic goal of a greater population of "racially fit" individuals.

If the National Socialists had merely employed these positive eugenic measures in the

The Holocaust

In the aftermath of World War II, many Hitler Youths had a great deal of difficulty coming to terms with the results of the race war in which they had willingly, if unknowingly, participated. Seeing the inside of the concentration camps was particularly difficult for many. The following is an account of the reactions of a Hitler Youth whose unit was shown Dachau by American soldiers. His reaction appeared in H. W. Koch's *The Hitler Youth*.

"To our left and right soldiers mingled with concentration camp inmates, the latter wearing the vertically blue-striped suits which hung on figures so thin that it was impossible to believe that these people could still speak, let alone walk. Their heads were either shaven or otherwise covered by a beret of the same material as the suits. The gate was flanked by two Sherman tanks, their crews sitting on the turrets and hulls feeding the surrounding men with chewing gum and chocolate and handing out cigarettes. . . . During the first few minutes after entering the compound I thought the inmates were going to tear us to pieces. Astonishingly enough, they just flanked the way wherever we went, but never a word was uttered, not a hand raised against us. First we were taken to a railway siding that branched off from the SS main camp. An American soldier selected a few of us (apparently the strongest-looking ones) and in perfect German ordered us to open one of the freight carriages on the siding. With metal bars and a good deal of effort we pushed back the doors.

The first thing that fell out was a skeleton of a woman. After that nothing more fell out, for the dead bodies were standing so close to one another, like sardines, that one supported the other. . . . Next we were taken to a red brick building enveloped by an acrid smell. We entered a hall and, for a moment, we thought we were in a boiler room with a number of big furnaces. That idea was immediately dispelled when we saw before each furnace a stretcher of metal with iron clamps. Some of these were still halfway in the furnace, covered by remnants of burned bodies. That night was a sleepless one. The impact of what we had seen was too great to be immediately digested. I could not help but cry."

One of the first groups of people killed by the Nazis in the Holocaust were people with disabilities. Quite a few U.S. citizens who lived and traveled in Germany either saw or heard about these killings. William L. Shirer, a war correspondent in Berlin, wrote the *Berlin Diaries*. The book discussed his observations and experiences in Berlin in the early stages of World War II. Portions of his book were condensed in the June 1941 issue of *Reader's Digest*.

"It is the story of the *Gnadenstod*—'mercy deaths.' 'Mercy killings' would be a better term. The story is simply that since last fall the Gestapo, with the approval of the German government, has been systematically putting to death the Reich's mentally defi-

cient. How many they have executed is known only to Herr Himmler and a few in Berlin. A trustworthy German has estimated the number at 100,000. I believe this figure is too high, but certainly it is into the thousands.

The origins of this peculiar Nazi practice goes back to last summer, when the idea was put up to Hitler. At first it was planned to have the Führer issue a decree authorizing the putting to death of certain mentally deficient persons. But it was decided that this might be . . . embarrassing to Hitler if it got out. In the end Hitler simply wrote a letter to the secret police, authorizing *Gnadenstod* where persons proved to be suffering from incurable mental or nervous diseases."

race war, there would have been no Holocaust. However, they also used negative eugenic measures, taking steps to decrease the population they viewed as "unfit." The Nazis defined two types of people as unfit: people who made the Aryan race impure and racial enemies. Aryans with hereditary illnesses, homosexuals, those considered politically unreliable, and Jehovah's Witnesses were thought to contribute directly or indirectly to impurities in the Aryan race. Jews, Gypsies, Russians, Poles, and many other races were considered racial enemies. The Hitler Youth learned that these peoples were trying to poison the Aryan race and/or destroy civilization.

In the Third Reich, the Nazis believed that the best way to decrease the populations of those they viewed as "unfit" was to stop them from reproducing. They reasoned that reproduction could be halted if every representative of these groups was killed, basically

causing extinction. To achieve these ends, they embarked on a systematic attempt to destroy all representatives of groups seen as a threat to the Aryan race. They "exterminated" people by the millions, and created concentration camps specifically for this purpose.

Perhaps the most significant contribution Hitler Youths made was their work in denouncing people. Hitler Youth members were told to watch for "unfit" people, or people who assisted the "unfit," and report them to Nazi officials. In her book *Frauen: German Women Recall the Third Reich*, author Alison Owings quotes a woman who went to her fortieth class reunion only to find out the reasons why some of her classmates had thought about denouncing her:

"She said to me, 'Did you really know that I wanted to report you?' Say I, 'Why? I can imagine that you wanted to report me a couple of times. Others reported me, too.' She said, 'Once you came to school and brought sort of a suitcase record player and brought *The Threepenny Opera* by Brecht [with the score by Kurt Weill] and during recess played [the records] and wanted to show us that this Jewish music is really very nice.'" (Brecht was not Jewish, but Weill was, and the songs were verboten [forbidden].)[31]

In other words, a young girl was nearly reported as unreliable for bringing the records of a Jewish composer to school. Her story highlights not only the extent to which any sort of association with Jewish people was forbidden in the Third Reich but also the fact that boys and girls went to great lengths, reporting their classmates and sometimes even their parents, to do their duty.

During World War II, the Hitler Youth also helped the Nazis expel "unfit" people from their homelands. When Germany conquered Poland, HJ and BdM members were called on to assist in "resettlement" and Germanization programs. This meant that native Polish people were forced to leave their homes, and some were "resettled" to concentration camps or were simply murdered. Native Germans went to live in their homes and in their country. The BdM and HJ helped remove the native Poles from their ancestral homes. Melita Maschmann, a former BdM leader, explained her unit's role in the resettlement of Poland:

> [The girls watched] as whole families were driven from their ancestral farms. And now, in addition, [they had] to intervene if these people, whose future was bleak, secretly tried to take their cherished possessions with them under the eyes of the people driving them out. . . . Sometimes I had no choice but to make the Poles unload one of the carts and then to specify exactly which things could be loaded up again and which must be left behind.[32]

These were some of the contributions of the Hitler Youth organization and its members to the race war in the Third Reich. Some members gladly, and even fanatically, contributed to this battle. It was this race war that was presented to Hitler Youths as a scientific fact of nature; as a battle that they must win for the sake of humankind. It was also the basis of other aspects of the Nazi ideology that boys and girls learned in the Nazi state.

3 | Ideology and Activities

To make their young members strong, Hitler Youth groups spent the majority of their time together engaged in athletic activities. Members played sports, participated in warlike games, swam, boxed, hiked, and marched. A *Pimpf* was expected to be able to march thirteen miles a day carrying an eleven-pound knapsack. These athletic activities were designed to make Hitler Youth members the strongest and toughest youth in the world. In fact, the Hitler Youth spent so much time marching that it began to cause health problems. A medical journal article at the time concluded that "too much is demanded of the feet of these boys and girls, who have to march on hard roads, [and] carry heavy burdens." [33]

The remainder of the time that boys and girls spent in the Hitler Youth was devoted to teaching them about Nazi ideology. In 1931 the Hitler Youth organization began to hold "evenings at home" (*Heimabende*). Every month Hitler Youth leaders received bulletins informing them about what material to cover at these weekly meetings. Generally, important days were highlighted and members were lectured about National Socialist ideology.

The ideology that young people learned at *Heimabende* and in the Hitler Youth used the Nazi belief in a race war as its jumping-off point. Enthusiasm for the group suggests that many young people were very dedicated to these ideas and to the Nazi state that would come into being as a result of them. Of course, it is impossible to calculate how many members actually believed the National Socialist ideology in its entirety. Most likely, this depended on the member's relationship with, and view of, his or her parents. Members probably believed bits and pieces of this worldview.

Anti-Semitism

The Hitler Youth were taught that the greatest threat in the race war was the presence of Jews in Germany. According to the Hitler Youth handbook, they were the only "foreign" race with whom the German people had direct contact. They were, therefore, the only group with whom it was possible to racially mix and pollute the hereditary bloodline of the Nordic race. However, Hitler Youth members were told that this was not the only threat that Jewish people in Germany posed.

The National Socialists believed that just as Aryans were culture founders, Jews were culture destroyers. Therefore, young members were taught that their attempts at good racial health went hand in hand with "a defensive warfare against mind and blood contamination by the Jews." [34] German Jews were presented as a tricky, clever, and evil race. Nazis said the Jews were attempting to rule the world and were actively trying to destroy the Aryan race. Boys and girls were told that Jewish people tried to disguise themselves as Aryans, and they were warned to be on the lookout for the "Jewish invasion."

As girls of the BdM look on, older members of the HJ begin a march. Younger Pimpfs were expected to march thirteen miles a day.

In an interview, Ellen Frey tried to explain how she thought about Jewish people as a young girl in the BdM:

> At the time there was after all, the propaganda. I remember it. I was just recently talking about it with my son. "The Jews," our parents always told us, "the Jews are *every*where. They're in the *theater*, at the highest positions. They're sitting everywhere and have us in the palm of their hand." That's what our parents told us. And that was the opinion. They're everywhere and sort of push us Germans aside and take the best jobs. I mean, the Jews are intelligent and all and naturally did a lot and. . . . One thought, perhaps it's very good if they leave, so we get a turn. We Germans. That was the opinion of us young girls then.[35]

As a result of these views, anti-Semitism, or hostility toward both ethnic and religious

Jews, was a central aspect of National Socialism. The experiences of Solomon Perel attest to this hostility. Perel was a Jewish boy who, through a series of coincidences, was able to pretend to be a Hitler Youth to save his life in Nazi Germany. He recalled the reaction of one of his comrades to a large poster of a "horrible-looking Jew." The Hitler Youth's "expression changed. His face flushed and his chin began to tremble. . . . He reached for his dagger and boasted, half in jest, half seriously, 'If only I had one of these Jews here right now!'"[36]

The Hitler Youth did not learn anti-Semitism only from books, organized activities were also held to reinforce the message. For example, the Hitler Youth might stand outside a Jewish shop to stop customers from entering, or they might smash the shop's windows as a group activity. Members also ransacked Jewish shops, tearing them apart and looting merchandise. In some cases, Hitler Youth members even participated in Jewish pogroms, or organized massacres. One infamous pogrom

The morning after Kristallnacht, a Jewish merchant begins to sweep up the shattered glass in front of his store.

remembered today as Kristallnacht (Crystal Night), took place on November 9, 1938. SA troops and various other Nazis, including Hitler Youths, burned Jewish synagogues, shops, and homes throughout Germany. Thousands of Jews were beaten and arrested.

The *Volk* Community

The Nazi belief in a race war also led to a new definition of the world and its citizens. In the world, countries are usually defined by borders. The National Socialists taught the Hitler

Youth that citizenship should instead be determined by blood. This is the concept of *Volk* that arose from the Nazis' belief in a race war. The *Volk* were members of the superior race of people, or all people of "pure German blood," most specifically, all Aryans. Since the Nazis did not consider Jews to be of German blood, members of a Jewish family that may have lived in Germany for centuries were no longer considered citizens. Also, people of color were not citizens. Citizenship was defined by blood and race alone.

The National Socialists' unique view of citizenship meant they completely disagreed with the political borders of the countries of the world. The Nazis defined the German territory as "every region of central Europe which [was] inhabited by Germans in more or less permanent settlements and has received its cultural imprint from the German people."[37] In other words, the *Volk* were not only in Germany. German blood existed within the politically defined borders of other countries. All of these *Volk* around the world were called the *Volk* community. If these places were predominantly of "German blood," the Nazis reasoned that they should, by racial right, be a part of Germany to give the superior race more lebensraum, or living space. Thus, Hitler Youth were taught that Germany's borders should not be drawn by politicians based on mutual agreement between countries, but instead by race.

Socialism and Nationalism

Socialism and nationalism were also important parts of what the Hitler Youth were taught. The socialism of the Hitler Youth and the Nazis was antiwealth, antisocial status, and anti-intellectual more than it was a solid, defined ideology on its own. Leaders told the Hitler Youth that wealthy people's lives were too easy—they were not fighters, strong and tough. Along with this came a dislike of intellectuals. The National Socialists taught that "a man, though scientifically little educated but physically healthy, who has a sound, firm character, filled with joyful determination and will power, is of greater value to the national community than an ingenious weakling."[38] Intellectuals were seen as sissies, and academic pursuits were identified as Jewish since the ability of the mind was far less important than the strength of the body in the view of the National Socialists. They argued that Germany had lost World War I because it had been filled with wealthy people and intellectuals who were too sissified to fight against the Jews and therefore allowed them to weaken Aryan society.

This belief in position by physical fitness and character—not intellectual ability, status, or wealth—was also combined with a call to youth to put their community's needs above their own. Every member was to march for the common good of the *Volk* community. In a speech to the Hitler Youth, Hitler told them to

learn, while you are still young, that life for you must mean sacrifice: sacrifice of your personal freedom, sacrifice of your free time, sacrifice of many of the small pleasures of life; sacrifices when you take on yourself charges, not for the individual, not for yourself alone, German boys and German girls, but for your small, and yet so great community.[39]

This idea of sacrifice for the *Volk* community also touches on another part of Nazi ideology, nationalism. To put it very simply, nationalism is a citizen's dedication to the interests of his or her nation. The Nazis defined their nation by race, calling it the *Volk* community. Therefore, their nationalism meant that the individual person was dedicated to the interests of the *Volk* community. The other aspect of Nazi nationalism was a belief

Anti-Semitism

Melita Maschmann became a high-ranking BdM member and head of its press department. Her book *Account Rendered,* is written as an open letter to her Jewish childhood friend. In it, she tries to explain her anti-Semitism.

"Rosel Cohn was a Jewish classmate of ours, but I did not really connect her with 'the Jews.' *Those* Jews were and remained something mysteriously menacing and anonymous. They were not the sum of all Jewish individuals, who included yourself [Maschmann's Jewish friend] or old Herr Lewy: they were an evil power, something with the attributes of a spook. One could

not see it, but it was there, an active force for evil.

As children we had been told fairy stories which sought to make us believe in witches and wizards. Now we were too grown up to take this witchcraft seriously, but we still went on believing in the 'wicked Jews.' They had never appeared to us in bodily form, but it was our daily experience that adults believed in them. After all, we could not check to see if the earth was round rather than flat—or, to be more precise, it was not a proposition we thought it necessary to check. The grownups 'knew' it and one took over this knowledge without mistrust."

German schoolchildren study the borders of Berlin. When it came to national borders, the Nazis taught that these should be drawn by race, not by politics.

that this individual devotion of all the *Volk* to the community would create a stronger, better community that then, in turn, would make life better for the individual.

To teach Hitler Youths the importance of their *Volk* community, the National Socialists suggested members participate in a form of a land service. Although not obligated to do so by any mandate or decree, every year young people between the ages of sixteen and eighteen were expected to help the *Volk* community. Boys were generally sent to assist rural families with the harvest, and girls helped out in the homes of mothers with many children. This was designed to teach young people about putting the needs of the community before their own.

The Leadership Principle

The Nazis wanted a society in which a person's position was decided by his or her physical abilities and not by wealth, intellectualism, or his or her parents' positions. They wanted all of these individual people working toward one goal. To achieve this, they founded their movement and government on what they called the leadership principle that required absolute obedience to superiors. The principle was based on the ideas of race that the Hitler Youth were taught. The National Socialists argued that the Germanic race was authoritarian and, therefore, the leadership principle was the best way to organize a society for the German race.

In her book *Tomorrow the World*, Ilse Mc-Kee describes the Hitler Youth *Heimabende*. She discusses both the meetings she attended as a BdM member as well as the meetings for boys.

"The evening classes (*Heimabende*) were conducted by young girls, usually hardly older than we were ourselves. These young B.D.M. leaders taught us songs and tried desperately to maintain a certain amount of discipline without ever really succeeding. . . .

We were of course lectured a lot on National Socialist ideology, and most of this went right over our heads. In most cases the young girl leader did not know herself what she was talking about. We were told from a very early age to prepare for motherhood, as the mother in the eyes of our beloved leader and the National Socialist Government was the most important person in the nation. We were Germany's hope in the future, and it was our duty to breed and rear the new generation of sons and daughters who would carry on the tradition of the thousand-year-old Reich.

The boys evening classes were run in exactly the same way and in the same building. Frequently we would all have to go to the auditorium, where some important personage would give a lecture on racial problems and the necessity of raising the birth-rate. He too would remind us of our duties as future fathers and mothers of the nation, and somehow I never managed to suppress a giggle when I looked at those spidery-legged, pimply little cockerels who were supposed to become the father of our children."

Girls at an evening class prepare signs asking for materials needed by the war effort. Before the war, Heimabende topics centered on motherhood.

Members of a Schaft *study a Nazi newspaper. Nazi ideology was a vital part in shaping the way that the Hitler Youth viewed the world.*

In the Hitler Youth each boy or girl was the member of a *Schaft*—or group of approximately 15 youths—and was responsible to his or her group leader. These leaders answered to the leader of the *Schar*, who was in charge of roughly three *Schafts*—around 50 youths. *Schar* leaders had to obey their superiors, who oversaw three *Schars*, or about 150 members. This structure continued all the way up to Baldur von Schirach, who then answered to Hitler.

The Hitler Youth learned that their social standing, occupation, and wealth would depend on their leadership capabilities. Those young people who showed potential went to three-week leadership schools where they were prepared to be group leaders or part of the administrative team of the Hitler Youth organization. Youngsters who showed even greater potential often attended elite schools to prepare them to be the future leaders of the Third Reich.

Belief in the leadership principle was just one of the many aspects of the Nazi ideology that boys and girls learned in the Hitler Youth. Participation in activities designed by the organization also gave them a chance to actively learn and embody these ideals. Their acceptance of this ideology, based on a belief in a bitter war between the races, meant that they looked at the world and acted in a unique way.

The School Day of the Hitler Youth

When the National Socialists came to power in 1933, they quickly took control of the schools and education. The school day for boys and girls, all of whom were soon required to be Hitler Youth members, became an extension of the National Socialist ideology. When the goal of education in Germany changed, so too did, the atmosphere in schools, the subjects that were taught, and the way they were taught.

When they came to power, the Nazis looked at the state of German education and came to the conclusion that two major problems existed: 1) it placed too much emphasis on the individual and not enough on the responsibility of the individual to the racial community, and 2) educators spent too much time educating the mind and not enough on physical and character education. According to the National Socialist minister of education, Bernhard Rust, these two problems created a weak nation in which men grew selfish and had poor judgment. To correct this deficiency, the National Socialists announced in 1933 that "education had to be founded on the principles of biological and racial science."[40]

The new goal of education in Germany was for young boys and girls "to be and remain strong and healthy" by becoming "aware of their duty to maintain their racial purity and to [pass it down] to succeeding generations."[41] Since the goal changed, so too did the school experience of Hitler Youth members who became students in the Third Reich, an experience unprecedented in history. Hitler told educators that to achieve this goal, the primary focus of education must be dedicated to convincing Aryan children of their superiority and encouraging the breeding of healthy bodies. Military preparedness—to defend the Aryan race and pass down its legacy to future generations—became a large component of the education of young people. The Nazis told teachers that "military education is not a special part of a general comprehensive education, but the centre of all our obligations as educators."[42]

Learning Environment

One of the first things the Nazis did to change schools was to make certain that all teachers supported their new goals for education. In the winter of 1933 all teachers of Jewish descent lost their positions. To ensure that the remaining teachers supported them, the National Socialists made membership in the National Socialist Teachers' League mandatory. Membership required instruction in the philosophy of National Socialism, the Nazi curriculum, and utilization of Nazi teaching techniques. Above all, it meant that every teacher also had to be a party member. Margarete Sasowski, the wife of a teacher, told of the plight of her husband and two other teachers who did not wish to join the league. The three men did not know what to do, Sasowski remembered:

Students learn marksmanship at a firing range. Military preparedness became a large component of German education.

Then the youngest said, "I'll say it's too expensive for me. . . . Then we'll hear and decide what we do." He did it and two days later . . . he said, "Karl [her husband], just join the old . . . Party. I've already gotten my transfer." They sent the poor fellow out of the village to a thing where he had to, God knows what else, fetch water. They gave him that kind of terrible job. That was thanks for his saying it was too expensive. Then the other [teacher] came to my husband and said, "What should we do?" . . . My husband said, "There's nothing else we can do or they'll do the same to us."[43]

In the first two years of Nazi rule, those teachers who were deemed unreliable or refused to join the league were dismissed. In one district alone 15 percent of male and 32 percent of female teachers were discharged. This way, Nazis could make certain that the atmosphere, materials taught, and teaching in schools were under their control.

Once the Nazis had gained control over the teachers, the National Socialist ideology became a part of the school atmosphere, and the school environment became hostile for Jewish students. In 1933 the Nazis passed the "Law Against the Overcrowding of German Schools and Universities." It put a quota on the number of Jewish or half-Jewish students a school could have. As a result, many Jewish boys and girls were asked to leave school. Those Jewish students who were still able to attend were harassed by classmates. At times, even the teachers participated in the harassment; some teachers refused to call on their Jewish students, others used these pupils as teaching aides, and still others physically harassed Jewish children. There was no way that Jewish students or their parents could stop this. Students either had to leave school or put up with the harassment.

This blatant anti-Semitism changed the school experience for Jewish youth, but it also changed the school environment for Hitler Youth members. Although anti-Semitism existed in schools before the Nazis came to power, it did not have the backing of the state. After 1933 it did. Hitler Youth boys and girls were encouraged by some classmates and teachers to be hostile toward Jewish children, and some learned to be anti-Semitic in the classroom. Then, in 1938, the National Socialists passed a second legal measure that excluded all Jewish children from schools. Jewish youth no longer had access to education, and the Hitler Youth no longer had any interaction with Jewish youth at school.

Anti-Semitism was not the only part of the Nazis' ideology that affected the atmosphere of schools. Their belief in the survival of the fittest did as well. The Nazis considered fighting good because it was thought to toughen up children. According to Nazi ideology, the strong were supposed to dominate the weak without mercy. In the case of some schools, this meant that more fighting with, and general harassment of, weaker students was tolerated.

The Curriculum

The curriculum of schools changed with the teachers and the learning environment. In a first-grade math class, counting, addition, and

The National Socialist School

Frederic Sondern Jr., a U.S. citizen, visited Germany a number of times before and after the Nazis came to power. He wrote an article that appeared in the September 1939 edition of *Reader's Digest* describing some of the changes he observed. He goes into some detail about educational changes in teacher training, curriculum and pedagogy.

"The six-year-olds do not write 'The cat is black' in their exercise books, but 'Adolf Hitler is my Leader.'... A little girl was caught lying. She had to write 50 times on the blackboard—'I am not pure Aryan and am therefore given to lying.'

At the age of 10, with secondary school, begins the really serious curriculum. The teachers must be 'politically reliable' and sponsored by their local party chieftains.... They must be graduates of the High School of Teacher Training, where the primary purpose is to create a 'soldierly' teacher. 'You teachers are Storm Troopers of German education, dedicated to the rearing of a . . . race,' said Minister of Education Rust in 1933. . . .

I have talked with a good many of these teachers. They know little outside of the textbooks which they have learned by heart. . . . [In the textbooks] all the problems have connection with National Socialist principles. There are endless arithmetic problems on airplanes flying at a certain speed with a certain load of bombs. . . . In physics problems . . . an aviator drops a bomb, or a soldier throws a hand-grenade. In geography, the pupils draw maps of the German Empire as it was and as it will be when the *Führer* completes it. The biology teachers prove that the German races are the finest in the world.

I was in a history classroom when a boy of 14 disputed the textbook description of the Battle of Jutland. His father had been in the battle and had told him about it. The boy received a whipping. And something infinitely worse—as the teacher told me later. 'We have marked it down in his Party Record.'"

subtraction might be taught. This is called the curriculum of the class, and it refers to the concepts and ideas covered by teachers and students in the classroom. When the National Socialists came to power, they created a new requirement—every student must take courses in racial biology—and began teaching the National Socialist ideology at every grade level. Ilse McKee, a schoolgirl at the time, noticed this curriculum change. She recalled that

a great change in the whole educational system took place. . . . Every subject was now presented from the National Socialist point of view. Most of the old lecture books were replaced by new ones which had been written, compiled, and censored by government officials. Adolf Hitler's *Mein Kampf* became the textbook for our history lessons. . . . A new subject, the science of the races, was introduced, and religious instruction became optional.[44]

In accordance with the new goals of education, immediately upon entering school at age six, boys and girls were taught about the superiority of the Nordic race and the inferiority of other races. Six year olds read fairy tales and stories about Hitler, sang songs about National Socialism, and were taught the beginnings of National Socialist ideology. Gregor Ziemer, the president of an American school in Germany, observed a variety of schools in Nazi Germany. One of his visits to an elementary school reading class illustrates the way one teacher taught students about the National Socialist concept of the natural struggle of life and the necessity for the strong to conquer the weak. The students recited the following poem:

"Please," begged the victim, "let me go,
For I am such a little foe."
"No," said the victor, "not at all,
For I am big, and you are small!"[45]

Another significant change in school curriculum concerned the way that history was taught. The goal of historical education in the Third Reich was in part to convert those who doubted or opposed the National Socialists. Historical texts presented a racial drama of history in which all events finally culminated in the ultimate German achievement—Adolf

Changes in the way that history was taught led some German students to believe that conquerors such as Genghis Khan were of Aryan descent.

Johannes Steinhoff, Peter Pechel, and Dennis Showalter's *Voices from the Third Reich: An Oral History* includes the account of Hanns Peter Herz. A half-Jewish boy in Nazi Germany, Herz tells of his friendship with a boy at school. His story illustrates both the friendships between Jews and non-Jews and the treatment of Jewish students by Hitler Youths in school.

"Starting after 1933 we didn't belong anymore. They broke our kitchen windows and the glass in our front door. On the wooden part of the door they scrawled a Star of David and wrote, 'Jews, get out!'

I started secondary school in 1938. The teacher put a boy beside me whom I found to be the most unlikeable person I'd ever met. Yet just four weeks later he was my best friend. He did a lot to help me get over this mentality of cringing and taking it all. You see, I was constantly being teased and beaten up by classmates—being called Jew, 'freak',

and so on. Then my friend started punching me until I learned to hit back. After that, I knocked a tooth out of the next guy who tried to beat me up; that stopped the beating for awhile. I was eleven years old.

The following year, something happened that I'll never forget, because it showed Nazis could have two sides. A boy named Lippert, the youngest son of the Nazi mayor of Berlin, joined our class; he sat right behind me. One day after recess—right before German class—I came back into the classroom and found a Star of David scribbled on my desk bench. And in the few minutes that I sat at my desk with my back turned, he wrote 'JEW' on the back of my jacket.

Our German teacher walked into the classroom. He saw it and came over to me, 'Stand up! Who did that?' I was afraid to tell on a high-ranking Nazi's son and said, 'I don't know.' 'Fine,' said the teacher, 'Then *you'll* get paddled.' My friend stood up and said, 'It was Lippert!' "

Hitler. What generally ended up happening was that any person who had a positive effect on history was determined to be an Aryan. One *Pimpf* came home to tell his father that he had learned that "Genghis Khan (a famous Mongolian leader who conquered Asia and obviously not a Nordic) must have been a Nordic, because no one but a Nordic could have done what he did." [46]

Textbooks focused on dramatically telling propaganda stories where Aryan heroes bravely fought to overcome evil Jewish influence. They told of brave young boys who "stormed singing to their deaths" [47] in World War I. They glorified dying for Germany and Hitler. They highlighted the Nazi belief that

all positive advances in history had been made by Aryans. The Nazis also used such stories to prepare young people for war by instilling in them a desire to be a hero by making a military sacrifice for the Third Reich. History became the ultimate academic tool to teach youngsters about Nazi ideology.

The National Socialist point of view also became part of other subjects. Even subjects such as math were infused with Nazi ideology. They used word problems like the following one to prepare youngsters for war: "A squadron of 46 bombing aeroplanes throws bombs at an enemy town. Every aeroplane carries 500 bombs weighing 1,500 kg each. Calculate the weight of all the bombs together." [48] In one

A Hitler Fable from an Elementary-School Book

The following is a story told to elementary-school children that was written by Baldur von Schirach. It is taken from a book titled *Fables for Elementary Students (Fibel für die Grundschule)* and is reprinted as it appears in George Mosse's *Nazi Culture*.

"Far from our homeland, our Führer Adolf Hitler has a beautiful villa. It is located high up in the mountains and is surrounded by an iron fence. Often many people who would like to see and greet the Führer stand in front of it.

One day the Führer came out once again and greeted the people in a very friendly way. They were all full of joy and jubilation and reached out with their hands to him.

In the very first rank stood a little girl with flowers in her hands, and she said in her clear child's voice: 'Today is my birthday.'

Thereupon the Führer took the little blond girl by the hand and walked slowly with her through the fence and into the villa. Here the little girl was treated to cake and strawberries with thick, sweet cream.

And the little one ate and ate until she could eat no more. Then she said very politely: 'I thank you very much!' and 'Good-by.'

Then she made herself as tall as she could, put her little arms around the Führer's neck, and now the little girl gave the great Führer a long, long kiss."

Hitler accepts flowers from a young admirer. Baldur von Schirach wrote a fable based on a similar event.

arithmetic book, students were asked to solve the following: "The Jews are aliens in Germany—In 1933 there were 66,060,000 inhabitants in the German Reich, of whom 499,682 were Jews. What is the percentage of aliens?"[49] Such math problems convey the Nazi belief that Jews were not Germans. Children began doing math and learning about war, anti-Semitism, and other aspects of Nazi ideology well before they joined the Hitler Youth.

The fact that all subjects were taught from the Nazi viewpoint was one of the most significant changes made in the curriculum of the schools. However, because the Nazis believed that it was more important to be physically fit than intellectually educated, they also asked schools to devote between two and five hours a day to physical education. The number of years each student was required to go to school was shortened, allowing young people to join the workforce or have children at a younger age. Likewise, Hitler Youth activities took precedence over school. For these reasons, children spent much less time in the classroom and less time on academic subjects such as reading, writing, math, science, history, and foreign languages. As a result, many schools stopped offering art classes, languages such as Latin or Greek, and even sciences other than racial science. The fact that many subjects were not taught at all represented a drastic change in the curriculum of German schools.

Prior to Nazi control, it had been the German teacher's duty to present knowledge and allow students to ask questions and discuss topics. After 1933, however, the Hitler Youth members were expected to listen to their teachers and to learn the curriculum without question. Boys and girls were told that there was one right way of thinking. This was the National Socialist way of thinking, and all other opinions were considered incorrect. Even when students were asked to write essays about their aim in life or why they belonged to the Hitler Youth, there was a single right answer. All others were wrong. Young people were not allowed opinions other than those of their teachers', and their teachers were not allowed opinions other than those embraced by the National Socialists.

The School Day of a Boy

The National Socialists believed that "the teaching of boys and girls, though of identical value, [should proceed] along different roads, which [was] necessary for the reason [of] respective spheres of men and women."[50] As a result, boys and girls did not have the same classes, at times were not in the same building, and always had very different school days. The Nazis wanted boys to be educated to prepare them to be good soldiers in the military, strong and obedient. Thus, the most important subject in a boy's day was physical educa-

tion, which would prepare him to defend his race. Each boy was required to participate in at least two hours of physical education a day.

Boys took part in all sorts of sports and gymnastics. Hitler suggested that one sport in particular would train young men to be strong, brutal guardians of the race: boxing.

There is no sport that, like this, promotes the spirit of aggression in the same measure, demands determination quick as lightning, educates the body for steel-like versatility. If two young people fight out a difference of opinion with their fists, it is no more brutal than if they [fence]. Also, it is not less noble if one who has been

A gymnast demonstrates his strength at a Nazi rally. The National Socialists believed that physical fitness should be the most important subject in a schoolboy's day.

attacked wards off his attacker with his fists instead of running away and calling for a policeman. But above all, the young and healthy boy has to learn to be beaten. . . . The folkish State has not the task of breeding a colony of peaceful aesthetes (artists) and physical degenerates.[51]

Bearing in mind Hitler's views, it is not surprising that boxing became an important part of the lives of young boys. They were taught the sport in school, and they were encouraged to settle their disputes through boxing. Beating someone up and being beaten up were considered necessary parts of National Socialist education. Therefore, teachers as well as Hitler Youth leaders tolerated fistfights among boys.

The second most important subject in a boy's day was character education. Boys were educated to be faithful to their race, to sacrifice themselves for the good of the *Volk*, to be courageous, to be obedient to leaders, and to have willpower. To accomplish this, Nazi textbooks, especially history books, contained stories of National Socialist heroes who had died for the cause. The stories of boys and men whose only claim to fame was that they died as National Socialists received entire chapters in textbooks. Their accomplishments were given as much attention as German political leaders and historical figures. The stories of these martyrs emphasized ideas of sacrifice, death, bravery, or racial purity perhaps to prepare boys for the war they would one day fight.

Young boys were also taught character fitness as part of science, math, and reading. Ziemer tells of a science class that he observed in which boys were taught about obedience and the leadership principle. The class had taken a field trip, and the teacher asked them to explain what they saw. Boys remarked that they had seen ants, beetles, and "two roosters fight." The teacher told the boys that "everywhere you looked . . . you saw . . . the principle of leadership. . . . Everywhere in nature the leader had to be obeyed; the strong dominated the weak."[52] This type of teaching, combined with the stories in Nazi textbooks, allowed character fitness to be taught in every subject.

Boys learn how to box— without gloves—during a physical education class.

The School Day of a Girl

The school day of a girl focused on teaching her to become a woman who would not "look upon the soldiering activities of [her] menfolk as a necessary evil, but as a sacred duty."[53] Girls were taught to be good mothers and wives who would gladly send their children and husbands off to war. The National Socialists wanted healthy mothers. They "wanted girls to feel that their bodies were more important for the State than their minds."[54] For this reason, physical education was also an important part of the girls' day. They participated in gymnastics and sports, but never in sports such as boxing. These warlike sports were for boys. It is also important to note that the intellectual education of girls was not valued. In fact, many girls were discouraged from taking academic classes and were encouraged to quit school to begin having children.

After physical education, two subjects were of equal importance for girls: domestic science and racial biology. In domestic science classes girls learned about cooking, housework, and gardening. At times, mathematics was taught as a part of domestic science. These classes were somewhat similar to today's home economics classes, except that the focus was on how to make a nice home for their future husband. The girls also spent a great deal of time learning racial biology. They had up to two courses a day in this "science." They learned about the importance of racial purity, the superiority of the Nordic race, infant care, and how to manage a family. The courses also contained detailed instruction in sex education. Girls learned about reproductive organs, conception, and childbirth all in an attempt to make them better mothers of the Aryan race.

Schoolchildren salute their teacher on their way to class.

The schools also encouraged girls to do what they could for the war effort. In domestic science classes, they were instructed about how to cook healthy foods during shortages. They were told of their opportunities to assist the Red Cross and in air protection. However, they were told again and again that their most important role was to give birth to the future soldiers of the Third Reich.

At age fourteen, young Germans could decide to leave school. The vast majority chose to do just that, either beginning a family, working, or becoming an apprentice. Therefore, while most members of the Jungvolk and Jungmädel spent their days in school, the greater part of BdM and HJ spent their days working either at a job or in the home. Those who stayed in school until the age of eighteen could get their *Arbitur* (diploma) and then could go on to college after completing their labor and military services for the Third Reich. However, between the ages of six and fourteen every boy and girl belonged in school—schools controlled by the National Socialists and expected to prepare students for their future role in the Third Reich, be it soldier or mother.

Home Life

Hitler Youth members had lives outside of school. They went home to families where they were not only Hitler Youth members or students but also sons and daughters, brothers and sisters, and grandchildren. In this context there were different expectations. Parents expected their children to obey, to do chores, to grow into adulthood. Members also had social lives that included activities, friendships, and dating. Their membership in the Hitler Youth, as well as their existence in the Nazi state, greatly influenced these relationships since the Nazi leadership intervened in family life to such a great degree that it even told parents what to buy their children for birthdays.

The Hitler Youth vs. Parents

Although the National Socialists spent a great deal of time talking about their respect for the "holy bond" of the family, this was true only if the parents believed in the National Socialist program. In reality, the Hitler Youth organization and the ideology it taught often caused a rift between parents and children. The most obvious cause of conflict was that some parents rarely saw their children. Hitler Youth boys and girls would leave for school in the morning, and at times they would not return until late in the evening. This schedule was especially difficult for farm families. One farmer remarked to his daughter, "If the children all went to Hitler Jungend (*Jungvolk*

and HJ) and the Bund deutscher Mädel (BdM), who is going to be doing work at home?"[55]

In families where the mother and father also belonged to party organizations, this problem was even greater. Although the Nazis talked about the family, if each family member did what the Nazis asked him or her

In this propaganda photograph, a girl helps bring in the harvest on the family farm. In reality, the requirements of the Hitler Youth and BdM left little time for chores.

to do for the party, they would rarely see each other. This was the topic of a popular joke about the father in the SA, the mother in the Nazi Women's Organization, the Frauenschaft, the son in the HJ, and the daughter in the BdM who only got to see each other once a year at the party rally.

The time taken up by various Nazi organizations was not the only problem for families. Families in which parents did not agree with the National Socialist ideology faced even greater obstacles. The Nazis were hostile toward these parents. Hitler alluded to this early on in a 1933 speech: "When an opponent says, 'I will not come over to your side,' I calmly say, 'Your child belongs to us already. . . . You will pass on. Your descendants, however, now stand in a new camp. In a short time they will know nothing else but this new community.'"[56]

For some parents who disagreed with the Nazis, this became all too true. If their children did not join the Hitler Youth, the parents faced fines or possible imprisonment. In the organization, as well as in school, young people were exposed to a great deal of National Socialist propaganda; as a result, young people tended to be greater believers in the Nazi ideology. One woman did not even trust her own daughter, stating simply that "children today are so different."[57] This put a great deal of stress on relationships between parents and children. In his book *A Social History of the Third Reich*, Richard Grunberger points out that

> mother and son relationships were particularly affected. Ten-year-old lads who were awarded daggers not surprisingly entertained vastly inflated notions of their self-importance, and many a mother's patience was sorely tried by a pre-adolescent 'Master in the House' for whom the thought of

having to defer to the authority of mere women seemed unnatural.[58]

However, a son disobeying his mother was not the only problem that came between parents and children as a result of the Hitler Youth organization. Some parents had their children taken away from them by the local Hitler Youth office because they were "politically unreliable." Some of the offenses for which parents lost their children were "friendship with Jews, refusal to enrol (*sic*) children in the Hitler Youth, and membership in the Jehovah's Witnesses."[59]

Parents vs. Children

Under these conditions it is not surprising that family relationships were strained when parents did not agree with the Nazi program. Many parents simply became very cautious about speaking around their children. This was not necessarily because they feared that their children would turn them in, but they worried that a child might innocently repeat something to a Hitler Youth leader or member who would label them unreliable and take away the child.

However, some parents did fear their own children. At times children denounced their own parents. Stories circulated in the Hitler Youth of young people who had turned their parents over to the authorities because they were politically unreliable and then were promoted to leadership positions because of their loyalty to the National Socialist cause. Alfons Heck recalls that "Walter Hess, a minor Hitler Youth leader, acquired a certain amount of fame and a promotion for reporting his own father directly to the *Gestapo*. It appeared *Herr* (Mr.) Hess, once a Communist, had called the *Führer* a blood-crazed maniac and scolded his son for his allegiance.

Inmates stand at attention at Dachau. Some Hitler Youths saw their parents placed in concentration camps such as this because of partial Jewish heritage or political unreliability.

Herr Hess was arrested the same night and sent to Dachau, where he died."[60] The fact that things such as this occurred is a testament to just how much some young people believed Nazi ideology.

At times parents were taken from their children. This was especially true in the case of Hitler Youth members who had parents who were legally classified as being of Jewish descent. In the Third Reich, someone was considered to be of mixed Jewish blood if he or she had one full-blooded Jewish grandparent. Therefore, the parent of a Hitler Youth member could be legally considered to be of Jewish descent although the child was not because she or he had no full-blooded Jewish grandparents. As a result, some Hitler Youth members saw their parents arrested and taken away for being Jewish. Parents were also arrested and taken from their children for being politically unreliable.

Religion

Parents and children also had great difficulty dealing with the Hitler Youth organization when it came to religious worship. Religious people and organizations were placed in precarious positions in 1933. The National Socialists claimed unlimited power in Germany, especially over its youth. The Nazis viewed Christianity, and especially Christian youth groups, as competing with them in their attempts to "own" German youth. Although it was still possible to practice Christianity in the Third Reich, it was difficult to be part of a youth group. Also, the schedule of the Hitler Youth at times made it impossible to attend evening or weekend church functions. In this way, Christian worship was made more difficult for young people in Germany.

Prior to 1933 many boys and girls belonged to religious youth groups. The National Socialists did not want any competition when it came to youth membership in the Hitler Youth, however, so they began to ban and dissolve these youth groups. In Germany, Christian youths were either Protestants or Catholics. Of these two groups, the Protestants were more easily dealt with by the Nazis.

Some Protestant boys and girls joined the Hitler Youth by choice or were encouraged to do so by their church groups. A statement by the Protestant youth leadership informed young people that "we thank God for this wonderful turning-point in German history, which he has carried out throughout the Reich Chancellor Adolf Hitler."[61] Those Protestant youths who did not immediately choose to join slowly began to lose their church groups during the *Gleichschaltung*.

The remaining Protestant youth groups succumbed to the Hitler Youth organization in December 1933, when the Protestant Church came to an agreement with the Nazis. The terms of this arrangement were that "Protestant Youth movements accepted uniform political instruction by the National Socialist state and the Hitler Youth. All members under the age of eighteen were to

The Rift Between Parents and Hitler Youths

The Nazi ideology that boys and girls were taught in school and in the Hitler Youth at times conflicted with the beliefs of their parents. In *Voices from the Third Reich*, editors Johannes Steinhoff, Peter Pechel, and Dennis Showalter include an account of Albert Bastian, who was six years old when Hitler came to power. He wrote the following about the rift that developed between him and his parents following the Crystal Night pogrom:

"I was ten years, ten months, and eighteen days old when I had to make my first political decision. It was the morning after Crystal Night, the night of November 9, 1938, when all the synagogues in Germany went up in flames; when the windows of countless Jewish shops were smashed by the National Socialists; when thousands of Jews were arrested and taken to concentration camps.

It was still dark outside when I woke and heard a strange man's voice coming out of the kitchen. A stranger in our house in the middle of the night?

It was Levi, the Jewish livestock dealer to whom my father always sold the calves; the Jew who supplied us with pork lard all year and always said to my mother, 'Ma'am, if you don't have money now, pay what you can, there's no rush. Your boys need some-

thing to chew on.' A Jew, a Jew—it kept running through my head. I was not at all happy that he was sitting in our kitchen. . . .

I had already been a member of the *Jungvolk* for ten months. In our small village on the French border, the leader of the *Jungvolk* group was our teacher. He had already talked to us about the Jews: 'The downfall of Germany in the First World War. You have to fight them wherever you can. . . .' We boys had the task of convincing our parents not to do business with Jews. And here was this Jew sitting in our kitchen. Levi wanted to get away to France. He had already sent his family to safety there in the spring of 1938.

I was in despair. Although my father opposed my teacher and refused to buy me a brown shirt, I respected my teacher. He was big and strong. 'The Führer,' my teacher said, 'expects you boys to be quick as greyhounds, tough as leather, and hard as Krupp steel.' And here was my father, a friend of Jews. I just couldn't figure it out.

When it got dark, my father took Levi across the border. When he came back my mother asked him, 'Are you sure nobody saw you?' 'You can rest assured,' my father told her, and at that moment I saw a smile light up my mother's face. And for the first time in my life I wished I wasn't my parents' son."

be integrated into Hitler Youth formations. The only concession made to Protestant Youth was that two afternoons a week should remain free for the educational activity of the church."[62] In the end, this concession meant very little since Hitler Youth membership took up so much time, and two afternoons were never actually free. Thus, the first thing the National Socialists did to infringe upon the worship of young people was to leave them no time to do so. In the end, boys and girls were left with only the scant time they had at home to worship.

The National Socialists had a greater difficulty dissolving Catholic youth groups. This was in part due to the fact that Catholicism is an international organization with a definite leader, the pope. This made Catholic groups far more powerful than the German Protestant Church, whose power was split leaving no clear leader. On July 30, 1933, Hitler negotiated a new concordat, or agreement, with Pope Pius XI. In exchange for the pope's support of the new Nazi government, Hitler agreed to guarantee people's freedom to practice Catholicism. Article 31 determined the destiny of Catholic youth groups, giving exclusively religious organizations the right to exist and assuring time off for Catholic Hitler Youth members on Sundays and on holy days.

However, as in the case of Protestant youth, these concessions were also quickly done away with by the National Socialists. Both the Nazis and the Roman Catholic Church had to agree on which organizations were to be considered "exclusively religious." This resulted in a great deal of bickering over which organizations fit the definition. In the end, the 1936 Law Concerning the Hitler Youth, and the 1939 decree enforcing it, put an end to most Catholic youth groups because, much like Protestant youth, young Catholics no longer had time to spend in these organizations or to worship.

The Nazi Religion

Some historians and academics have suggested that in some ways Nazism became a religion for young people during the Third Reich. In his book *German Youth: Bond or Free*, Howard Becker explains the reasons why he believes this to be true of some Hitler Youths in Germany.

"Religion? Of course. Any value-system for the sake of which its devotees sacrificially live and gladly die is a religion, regardless of whether or not it has a god in the traditional sense. Granting that Hitler is the earthly god of the Nazis, it is . . . true that he achieved his . . . position only because he visibly . . . embodied values which German youth had long been holding dear. . . .

The religion sought a prophet, and he (Hitler) then became its god. Once godhead had been accomplished, the alternatives that once existed were wiped out. . . . The only problem for the priests (Nazis) of the new religion was the defining of the creed and the standardizing of its ritual so that the greatest possible number of adherents could be gained and the dissenters cast into outer darkness. . . .

The ideologists and propagandists in the tow of Hitler skillfully perverted the new religion of German youth in ways which eventually led them to rush, like [pigs], down a steep place into the sea. Thorough regimentation, militarization, and enthusiastic support of and participation in the Second World War represented that rush."

Pope Pius XI agreed to support the Nazi government if Germans were allowed to practice Catholicism.

In the countryside the youth dedication ceremony (for the Hitler Youth) had little significant impact. . . . The majority of schools showed no interest in the dedication ceremony.[63]

The Nazis worked to further weaken Christian worship by teaching young people from a very young age that the ideal National Socialist had no religion but Nazism. They were careful not to go too far, though, because some Germans were quite religious, and they did not want to have any problems on their hands. However, to be a part of the SS, the most elite formation made up of only the best, ideal Nazis, a man had to renounce his religion.

Finally, the Nazis attempted to replace Christianity with National Socialist ideology in the lives of youth. Some National Socialists expressed discontent with the so-called Jewish roots of Christianity, namely that Jesus was a Jew. The Nazis began to remove Christian symbols, such as the cross, from schools. They also began to use Christian prayer and ritual in schools and children's activities to their own advantage. These prayers and rituals were altered in a very important way, however. Instead of praying to or thanking a Christian God, the children were doing so to the National Socialist state and the Führer. In these prayers it was Hitler, not Christ, who was the savior. The following is an example of one such "Hitler prayer." Children in the Cologne area were required to say this prayer to receive their free lunch:

Nonetheless, in predominantly Catholic areas of the Third Reich, the Nazi party and the Hitler Youth continued to compete with the Catholic Church. In some areas the Catholic Church was able to retain its hold over youth. In the town of Eichstätt, the Catholic Church appears to have been quite strong, much to the dissatisfaction of one official. A report dated June 20, 1944, discussed the excitement of young people for the Catholic holiday of Corpus Christi and their lack of enthusiasm for the Nazi youth dedication ceremony:

The Corpus Christi procession followed the usual traditional church ceremony. The procession, which was held on Sunday in Eichstätt, was notable for the large number of young people who took part.

Führer, my Führer, bequeathed to me by the Lord,
Protect and preserve me as long as I live!
Thou hast rescued Germany from deepest distress,
I thank thee today for my daily bread.

During a rally held in Munich, members of the Hitler Youth rest together under a tent. The Nazis wanted to create a spirit of comradeship between all Aryan children.

Abideth thou long with me,
forsaketh me not, Führer, my Führer,
my faith and my light!
Heil, mein Führer![64]

This type of Hitler worship affected the religious worship of both Catholic and Protestant youth since they were being taught to revere Adolf Hitler as though he were a god. This contributed to some boys' and girls' adoration and fanaticism about Hitler and the Nazis, and it created tension in families in which parents remained loyal to a religion that had been replaced by Nazism in their children's lives.

In the case of Jewish youth, the Nazis were not interested in converting them to Nazi ideology. When the Nazis came to power, Jewish youth groups were placed in an unenviable position. These groups were left intact, but only because Jewish boys and girls were not eligible for Hitler Youth membership. Indeed, the Nazis dissolved Jewish youth groups for very different reasons. The groups were left alone between 1933 and 1937. In his book *The German Youth Move-*

ment, 1900–1945, Peter D. Stachura discusses the work and the fate of these youth groups:

The emphasis in Jewish youth work lay in the preparation and dispatching of members to settlements in Palestine. The youth groups performed in this regard an important role in saving thousands from the terrible fate which lay ahead at the hands of the Third Reich. . . . [In November 1938] Jewish youth groups . . . were banned and dissolved. . . . [For those members who had not gone to Palestine,] there was the option of organizing underground resistance to the regime . . . or simply waiting for further degradation and finally extermination.[65]

In other words, the elimination of Jewish youth groups had nothing to do with competition with and dissolution by the Hitler Youth organization. It was a by-product of the Nazi drive to eliminate Jewish people from Germany.

Friendships

The National Socialists attempted to make the Hitler Youth the ideal expression of the *Volk* community. They wanted to create a spirit of comradeship between all Aryan boys and girls regardless of class. To accomplish this, they attempted to break down class distinctions. They took drastic measures when cliques arose along class lines within the Hitler Youth. In one such case, a group of upper-middle-class boys formed their own clique and tried not to associate with their working-class comrades. When the Hitler Youth leadership found out, the boys were "sent to 'Coventry' and for three months [they] had to devote their entire spare time, weekends included, to carrying out chores for working-class families where the father was a soldier."[66]

Such actions discouraged cliques, but they still could not create the ideal world of comradeship the Nazis desired. The fact was

Catholicism and Nazism

Following the passage of the Law Concerning the Hitler Youth, many young people who were not already members of the Hitler Youth had to seek membership. Stefan Heym wrote an article for the June 27, 1936, edition of the *Nation*. The article, "Youth in Hitler's Reich," expressed concern for these boys and girls. It included an account of some National Socialist actions against Catholic youth groups, and a story about a town coming together to protect its Catholic priest.

"Besides the boys and girls who for one reason or another have not yet joined the Hitler Youth but who will now be forced into the new youth service, there is one large group that has not been 'coordinated'—the Catholic youth organizations. Catholic youth have been protected by the Concordat with the Pope. But a totalitarian state cannot allow any other organization to exist—'who controls youth controls the future'—and the general fight against the Catholic church strikes especially at its youth organizations. On November 19, 1935, the central office of the Catholic Youth in Düsseldorf was occupied by the secret state police (*Gestapo*), searched, closed, and sealed. Some days later the Catholic Youth magazine *Michael*, which had a circulation of 300,000, was suppressed, and its offices sealed. Members of the Catholic youth organizations are forbidden to wear uniforms. Street battles between them and the Hitler groups occur almost daily in the Catholic regions, especially in the Rhineland.

One little episode from this fight: the priest of a town in the Saar had said that the race hatred of the Nazis is immoral. The local Nazi leader mobilized some members of the Hitler Youth and sent them to demonstrate before the house of the priest. The Catholic Youth of the town rallied thousands of people by ringing the big church-bell for an hour and a half. Catholics, Socialists, Communists came from all sides of the town to protect the priest. Meanwhile, the mayor had aroused the local S.A., but the S.A. refused to attack a crowd made up of their friends and neighbors. In the end, police had to be called from Saarbrücken, but they came too late, for the crowd had melted away, and everything was quiet. The priest was unharmed."

that boys and girls did not always make friends with all of the members of their Hitler Youth groups. They tended to form their deepest friendships based on who lived close to them and who went to school with them. Neighborhood and school friends tended to be of similar class status. Thus, although cliques were not allowed to form, boys and girls continued to play with their closest friends, and the National Socialists were never able to completely create the classless community they envisoned.

Social Life

Outside of school, the Hitler Youth organization, and their family obligations, boys and girls had very little free time. In the time they did have, Hitler Youth members engaged in a variety of activities, some legal, some not. Boys and girls played sports or games with friends, and going to movies was very popular, especially in the city, where there were theaters. Since the Nazis controlled what films were made, the movies that the Hitler Youth saw tended to reinforce the Nazi ideology they learned in school. Many showed Aryan characters triumphing over stereotypes of evil Jews and helped the National Socialists further indoctrinate the Hitler Youth.

Dating was also part of the lives of Hitler Youth members. Melita Maschmann, a former BdM member, recalled that "there was very probably a good deal of flirting during youth group activities, especially when boys and girls

were working together."[67] Some local Hitler Youth organizations planned social mixers for boys and girls. However, interaction between boys and girls, such as dating, typically occurred outside of the Hitler Youth since their formations were frequently separated.

Another common, but not always legal, pastime for the Hitler Youths, especially among the HJ and BdM, was watching adult films, smoking, and drinking at pubs. This became a problem as the war went on, and the Nazis took legal measures. The 1940 "Law for the Protection of Youth" "banned young people under eighteen from the streets after dark, as well as from frequenting restaurants, cinemas or other places of entertainment after 9 p.m. (if unaccompanied by an adult), and young people under sixteen from being served with spirits or smoking in public."[68] In order to get around this law, some boys and girls obtained fake documents on the black market that said they were older. However, HJ and BdM members who were over sixteen did go out drinking and smoking together in their free time, even though the Hitler Youth preached health and purity.

Thus, the National Socialists were able to seize control over many aspects of the home life of youth and strained a variety of relationships during the Third Reich. However, the Nazis were never able to have the total control they desired. Some Nazis reasoned that this was a result of parental and maybe even school influence, and they attempted to create situations in which this influence could be lessened or eliminated.

CHAPTER 6

The Complete Hitler Youth Experience

The Hitler Youth organization influenced the lives of all members. The majority of these boys and girls had other influences as well, including parents and school. However, there were times and places where the National Socialists took over the complete education and even the parenting of youngsters. This occurred in a variety of boarding schools that were established by the Nazi state and/or the Hitler Youth. In these schools youngsters lived, breathed, and embodied Nazi ideology without parental influence or interference.

National Political Education Institutions

In the Third Reich, two different types of schools trained the elite, future leaders of the Nazi state: the National Political Education Institutions and the Adolf Hitler Schools. Both were boarding institutions that accepted distinguished boys after their second year in the Jungvolk. Since the National Socialists believed that girls should be educated to fulfill the role of mother, few elite schools were established for them. A few were formed once the war broke out and the National Socialists realized that girls could be mobilized for duties other than motherhood. For the most part, however, elite education focused on making boys into soldiers and leaders.

The National Political Education Institutions, or Napolas, as they were called, were similar to military schools and were actually modeled after the cadet academies that had existed in Germany for many years before the Nazis came to power. The Napolas worked to completely indoctrinate their students into Nazism. They were dedicated to producing the elite Nazi who would be able to assume a leadership position in any area of German society—academic, military, or governmental.

Gaining admission into the Napolas began with preselection. To qualify, a boy had to be a Hitler Youth member, 100 percent Aryan, in excellent health and physical condition, good at paramilitary training such as marching and shooting, and have the support of his teachers and the sponsorship of the local Party chief. An application was submitted for boys who met these requirements. Applications for admittance were supposedly initiated by the boy's parents, but in practice this was not always the case. A Jungvolk member could be nominated without the approval of the boy or his parents. Once the nomination occurred, the family was notified but had no control over the selection process. If the boy was selected, he would have to leave home to attend, which greatly strained families that relied on their sons either for farm labor or for the wages they brought home.

Once a boy was preselected for admission, he underwent a week-long examination with all of the other preselected candidates. During this week, he took examinations in mathematics, grammar, and a variety of other subjects to help gauge his academic abilities. An equal amount of testing was done to

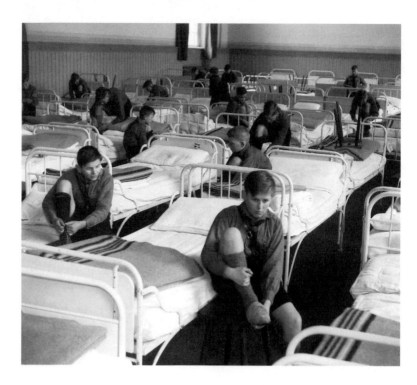

Hitler Youth dress in their Napola dormitory. Once boys were selected as students, they left home and went to live on campus.

determine the boy's physical prowess. Tests for physical capabilities included:

> swimming . . . athletics, obstacle races, and field exercises which included map reading. Part of the field exercise test was also carried out at night, usually taking the form of a para-military exercise, the capture of a defended forest bridge, or being dropped from the sidecar of a motor-cycle miles from anywhere and being ordered to make one's way back in the dead of night in totally unfamiliar territory.[69]

Throughout the testing period, the mental, emotional, and physical qualifications of the boys were carefully evaluated by selectors. Parents might also be interviewed in an attempt to gather more information about the competence of a candidate. Finally, after all of the boys were evaluated, the future students were selected from the pool of candidates.

Once boys were selected as students, they left home and went to live on campus. These twelve-year-old Napola students were now influenced by the National Socialist ideology twenty-four hours a day, seven days a week. Napolas taught students the same curriculum they would receive in any other school, but they also placed great emphasis on sports, especially sports that focused on paramilitary skills such as shooting, gliding, war games, and driving.

The daily schedule of a Napola student differed somewhat from that of a student attending a traditional school. Traditional schools generally taught academics in the morning and left the afternoon open for athletics and Hitler Youth activities. In comparison, the Napolas alternated between physical and academic education throughout the day. This schedule reflected the Napolas' concept of education. They wanted boys to realize that all types of education were equally important, and combined to create the whole boy.

Perhaps the most unique aspect of the Napolas was that boys also did a great deal of community service work and traveling. Younger boys spent time working with farmers for part of the year, and older boys worked in factories or coal mines. If a boy in the Hitler Youth wanted to grow up to be a successful leader in the Nazi government, military, educational system, or any other area of German society, attending a Napola was one way to start down this path. He remained in the school until age eighteen to receive his

The Final Product of Elite Education

In a quote from Louis L. Snyder's *Encyclopedia of the Third Reich*, Hitler discusses what he sees as the final product of the National Socialist education.

"I begin with the young. We older ones are used up. We are rotten to the marrow.

But my magnificent youngsters! Are there any finer ones in the world? Look at these young men and boys! What material? With them I can make a new world.

My teaching will be hard. Weakness will be knocked out of them. A violently active, dominating, brutal youth—that is what I'm after. Youth must be indifferent to pain. There must be no weakness and tenderness in it. I want to see once more in its eyes the gleam of pride and independence and the beast of prey.

I will have no intellectual training. Knowledge is ruin to my young men. I would have them learn only what takes their fancy. But one thing they must learn—self-command. They shall learn to overcome their fear of death under the severest tests.

This is the heroic stage of youth. Out of it will come the creative man, the god-man."

Hitler salutes his "magnificent youngsters."

Arbitur, at which time he completed his mandatory military service. After this, he could attend college if he so desired. His elite education would create future opportunities for him in the Third Reich.

Adolf Hitler Schools

Another way to receive an elite National Socialist education was to attend an Adolf Hitler School. These schools were unique for one particular reason: in Nazi Germany schools were part of the state. This meant that they had to meet the standards of and report and answer to the Ministry of Science and Education. The Napolas, even though they were elite boarding schools, were also under the jurisdiction of the ministry. This meant that the teachers were selected based on their academic teaching abilities and not solely on their political party membership. However, Adolf Hitler Schools were operated outside of the rest of the educational system. Their teachers were all party members and were chosen for their politics. These schools did not answer to the Ministry of Science and Education, they answered only to Nazi Party officials.

The Adolf Hitler Schools were founded in 1937 when the leader of the Hitler Youth organization, Baldur von Schirach, and another Nazi official, Robert Ley, released an announcement that Hitler had ordered the creation of such schools for boys who had distinguished themselves in the Jungvolk. Selection for admittance into the Adolf Hitler Schools also began in the second year of the Jungvolk. *Pimpfs* were preselected primarily on their appearance. The most Aryan-looking members, those having blond hair, blue eyes, and other Aryan features, were chosen to be candidates for admission. The schools then conducted racial background ex-

aminations of potential students, and Hitler Youth doctors gave physical examinations. If a candidate passed these exams—and many did not—then he participated in a two-week camp designed to help select the next batch of students.

At this point, the selection process was similar to that of the Napolas. Candidates took part in a two-week camp in which they engaged in various activities. In the selection process for the Adolf Hitler Schools, the majority of these activities focused on the boy's physical fitness and toughness. This physical prowess was closely monitored and evaluated by his group leader, and the final

Napola students dig a trench as part of their community service. Boys also worked on farms, in factories, and in coal mines.

The Creation of the Adolf Hitler Schools

The Adolf Hitler Schools were created for the education of the future leaders of Germany. The following is the announcement of their creation and is reprinted in Jeremy Noakes and Geoffrey Pridham's, *Nazism, 1919–1945: A Documentary Reader.*

"The Führer has issued the . . . decree dated 15.1.1937 concerning the Adolf Hitler Schools of the NSDAP (Nazi Party). The NSDAP and the HJ have thereby acquired a new and immense task which extends beyond our own time into the distant future. Details about the AHS will not be published today. To avoid uncertainty, however, we announce the following principles:

1. The Adolf Hitler Schools are institutions of the HJ, which is responsible for running them. Teaching materials, curriculum, and teaching staff will be determined by the undersigned Reichs [leaders] for the Reich as a whole.

2. The Adolf Hitler Schools will contain six classes. Pupils will as a rule be admitted at the age of twelve.

3. Boys admitted to the Adolf Hitler Schools will have distinguished themselves in the [Jungvolk] and have been recommended by the responsible Party cadre leader.

4. Instruction at the Adolf Hitler Schools will be free of charge.

5. Supervision of the schools is part of the responsibilities of the Gaulieter [regional leader] of the NSDAP. . . .

6. After the successful completion of the school leaving examination the pupils of Adolf Hitler Schools may pursue any career in Party and State."

---

selection for the elite schools was made by a party official, usually the local district head (*Gaulieter*). The Adolf Hitler Schools' selection differed from that of the Napolas in an important way: Napola selection included academic ability, but the selection for the Adolf Hitler schools, for the most part, did not. These schools were known for selecting candidates primarily by appearance and physical ability, or in other words, by what the National Socialists considered "racial health."

Not surprisingly, the curriculum also focused on racial health. An Adolf Hitler School student spent most of his day strengthening his body and learning military skills. In the case of academic subjects, students were not given grades, and they did not have to write papers or take individual tests. Military discipline was a significant part of the curriculum, so much so that in 1937, an outside observer noted that "in the Adolf Hitler schools the boys are under iron discipline every hour of the day. Every movement must be strictly military."[70] Indeed, military discipline was such an important part of the education received at these schools that tasks such as marching and making beds up to military standards were treated as more important than academic pursuits such as calculus.

Not only were academic subjects considered less worthwhile, there was also little time for them since at least five hours every day was devoted to physical activities and exercises. The little intellectual education that did occur essentially consisted of teachers repeating propaganda slogans to their students—teachers who were chosen for their dedication to Nazi ideology and not for their academic abilities. In fact, the intellectual education was so poor in 1939 that a Nazi official declared

Two Adolf Hitler School students make their room ready for inspection. Military discipline was an important part of the education received at these schools.

that "the knowledge pupils can acquire at the Adolf Hitler Schools is in every respect inferior to that provided by the best upper schools."[71] Criticism such as this brought about some reforms in academic education at the schools. By 1941 the schools had improved a great deal, and by 1945 they would have taught equal amounts of academic and physical education. The National Socialists were no longer in power after 1945, however, so most of the time that the Adolf Hitler Schools were in operation, they worked to produce a student who was physically elite and intellectually inferior. They worked to create the ideal tough, obedient Aryan soldier.

Ordensburgen

The final piece of the National Socialist elite school puzzle was higher education and polishing at the Ordensburgen (Castles of the Or-

der). The Third Reich only lasted twelve years, and in that time the Ordensburgen never really defined a purpose and produced a graduating class with it in mind. Originally, Ordensburgen were conceived of as the destination of the most promising Adolf Hitler School graduates.

First, a candidate for admission had to complete six years in the Adolf Hitler Schools, between the ages of twelve and eighteen. Then, he had to undertake two and a half years of labor service and four years as a full-time party official. After this experience, and preferably once he was married, the young man could apply for admission into the Ordensburgen, the most elite schools of the Hitler Youth.

The Ordensburgen were originally designed to provide a three-to-four year course for future leaders to improve and polish their leadership abilities. They were essentially finishing schools for the future leaders of the Reich. However, there was never a graduating class that had gone through all three years.

When the war began, the Ordensburgen closed since all of their potential students were off fighting for Germany.

The KLV Program

Whereas the Napolas and the Adolf Hitler Schools were boarding schools for the elite Hitler Youth members, the Kinderlandverschickung (KLV) program had the same type of influence in the life of some average members. Originally, the KLV was created in 1934 as a program for urban children who became ill. Through the KLV program, these children could go to the countryside on vacation and recuperate. However, when World War II broke out, the purpose of the KLV camps

Dinner at an Elite School

By a chain of incredible events, Solomon Perel, a young Jewish boy, ended up attending an elite Hitler Youth school. Perel had to keep the fact that he was Jewish carefully hidden in order to save his life. He wrote about his experiences in his memoirs, *Europa, Europa,* which are also the basis of a feature film by the same name.

In his book, Perel describes his first meal at the elite school. His description aptly shows both how students lived as well as how every action played a role in their indoctrination into Nazi ideology.

"Conversation was interrupted by voice of the *Scharführer* [comparable to a staff sergeant] in the hall: 'Get ready to march to the dining hall in five minutes!'. . .

Each of the boys knew what he was supposed to do, and they quickly formed rows of four. The *Scharführer*, asked me not to line up with them, not yet. . . .

'Right, right, forward march!' the *Scharführer* barked. I was ordered to bring up the rear. . . .

Without any instructions, they spontaneously and enthusiastically started to sing. I knew these songs: '*Auf der Heide wächst ein Blümelein, das heisst Erika*' ['A Flower Grows on the Heath, It's Called Heather'] and '*Die Lorelei,*' and under my breath I hummed along. . . .

As we approached the dining hall, they started a new song with horrendous murderous verses: '*Erst wenn vom Messer spritz das Judenblut, dann geht's uns nochmal so gut*' ['We'll be even better off once Jewish blood spurts from our knives'].

They were singing this song on their way to a well-set table. . . .

Marching to this powerful rhythm, we arrived at the dining hall. The pride and joy of the school, it could accommodate up to a hundred students. There were paintings of Viking heroes, flaming swastikas, guns, flowers, and plows on the walls. Nobody sat down right away. They were all standing stiff and straight as pokers, their eyes directed toward a small gallery below the high ceiling at the front of the hall. There, behind a microphone, sat the home leader getting ready to speak. . . .

A deathly silence reigned. And then the home leader spoke; the acoustics of the hall, which were comparable to those of a cathedral, amplified his voice. . . . After a while, I picked up a few words: 'Keep the race pure . . . be strong . . . *Lebensrecht* [right to life]. . . .' I thought, It's nothing but Nazi jargon."

changed. The KLV was transformed into a program to evacuate children who were threatened by the war, children in border areas and in cities in danger of being bombed. The idea was that "young people who [lived] in areas subject to repeated air raid alarms should be sent to the other areas of the Reich on a voluntary basis."[72]

However, the leadership of the Hitler Youth organization also saw the KLV program as an opportunity to have even more control and influence over the lives of average Hitler Youth members. They could turn entire public schools into boarding schools and take over the whole life of the child. The KLVs camps became places where the "influence of parents and teachers would be gradually eliminated to the advantage of the [Hitler Youth organization's] educational claims."[73] By 1944 over thirty-five hundred KLV camps existed.

Two older members of the KLV program perform their chores at a camp in the countryside.

If an area was thought to be threatened, the local public grammar school was relocated to a KLV camp. Some of the teachers from the local school were assigned to the camp, where they worked jointly with Hitler Youth leaders to teach and take care of the students. Once the grammar school was relocated, parents who wanted their children to attend school had four choices: They could send the child to live with relatives and attend a school in a safer part of Germany, they could place the child in a private school in the threatened area, or they could send the child with his or her class to the KLV camp, or they could choose to keep their child at home.

Some parents, especially those who supported the Nazis, wanted their children to go to the camps. However, others were reluctant to send their children away in the middle of a war and felt that if the family died, then it should all die together. Parents who did not like the Hitler Youth organization were especially opposed to KLV education, feeling that it was another Nazi attempt to take their children from them. Although the Nazis could not force parents to send their children, mothers and fathers were probably influenced by the fact that their children could not receive an education unless they attended their local school, which had been relocated to a KLV camp.

Similarly, some children were genuinely excited to attend the camps. However, there were other reasons why children asked their parents to go. One former *Pimpf* recalled that even though he disliked the Hitler Youth, he begged his mother to send him to the KLV camp instead of to live with his rural relatives. Although his mother pleaded with him not to go to the camp, he recalls that he did not want to transfer to a rural school because "I was afraid of being with new children who would probably tease me about my stuttering even

Many KLV camps were in conquered territories as part of the Nazi attempt to resettle and Germanize the areas. In these camps far away from their families, some Hitler Youths witnessed terrifying incidents. In *A Hitler Youth in Poland*, Jost Hermand tells of one such incident that he witnessed when in a KLV camp in Warthegau.

"I do remember one dreadful occurrence through which we, in the most gruesome way, became aware of the Germanization policy prevailing in the Warthegau. It must have happened in November or December 1943, because it was already very cold. One afternoon we were in the school courtyard when we saw an SS man on a bicycle coming from Standau (Straszewo), his dog running alongside. Because there was so little variety in our bleak schedules, some of us decided to run after him. We saw him suddenly stop and order his German shepherd to jump at a very pregnant Polish woman walking on the village street. The dog obeyed. The woman, probably a maid who worked for one of the German farmers, was very large and already somewhat awkward; with a scream she fell on her back and stared up at the growling dog in great fear. The SS man got off his bicycle and stomped on the woman's belly with his boots until she died from internal injuries.

I no longer remember what went through my mind during this incident, taking place as it did right before our eyes. It was probably a terrible mixture of fear, horror, pity, curiosity. . . . We never asked ourselves why it had happened. We knew only that the woman was unmarried, and so she had committed a 'sin.' There was no way we could have suspected that she might have been one of those Polish women who according to National Socialist policy were not permitted to reproduce. . . . I know only that afterward we felt extremely embarrassed and ran back to camp. We never talked about the incident again for fear of coming under suspicion of having been accomplices. We all knew something dreadful had happened. Yet we weren't able to fit what we had just experienced into our very limited view of life."

more than the boys in my school . . . so I implored her just as insistently to let me go to camp with my class."[74] Indeed, childhood fears such as having to start a new school and not wanting to appear to be a sissy or scared to leave home probably influenced the choices of young people.

Life in the KLV Camps

If children entered the KLV program, they left their homes and families and traveled to other parts of Germany. Six to ten year olds were housed with rural families, but children who were ten to sixteen were usually placed in KLV camp communities in the countryside. School buildings, hotels, youth hostels, and other facilities, including palaces and sanatoriums, were used for these communal camps.

There is some dispute about the atmosphere of the KLV camps, and most likely it differed from camp to camp. After all, around a million boys and girls attended more than thirty-five hundred camps. Therefore, even personal accounts that seem to contradict each other are probably in some ways true. Some adults have positive recollections of their time as children in KLV camps. One former student said,

> We had enough free time. On hot days we used it to bathe in one of the fountains in the inner park of the palace. Some of us were allowed to use the pony trap. In the autumn we used to roast potatoes on an open fire and in winter we went sledging [sledding]. We had brought our own skis and skates. There were cosy theatrical performances and numerous sports competitions in the outer courtyard.[75]

However, not all accounts of KLV camps are positive. Some former students tell of horrible living conditions where "mice and rats ran round the rooms."[76] Jost Hermand, a former KLV student, wrote a book titled *A Hitler Youth in Poland*. It is a direct response to those who believe that all KLV camps were wonderful accomplishments. He maintains that some camps were places where young people were exposed to a great deal of physical, sexual, and emotional brutality. According to Hermand, in some of the camps that he attended, young people were punished harshly for small offenses, "just because [a boy] whispered something to [his] neighbor . . . [he] could be locked up in the smoke room in the attic of the school building—a dark cubicle that could only be entered on one's knees and by ducking one's head. Because of the lack of fresh air, [a boy] couldn't last more than an hour and a half."[77]

Hermand also contends that in some camps the strong ruled over the weak without interference. The National Socialists did not believe in protecting the weak, and this allowed stronger bullies to terrorize weaker children twenty-four hours a day in some camps. One former student admits that the boys in his camp "behaved very badly. . . . Sometimes a boy would wake up and cry at night. We didn't behave in a very friendly way towards these chaps. Sometimes, it ended quite harmlessly with a pillow fight but sometimes also with a beating up for the person concerned. Yes, unfortunately one had to admit we were pretty merciless."[78]

KLV students enjoy a meal in camp. Some youths had positive experiences in the program, but others endured horrible living conditions and abuse.

Ready for inspection, KLV students stand at attention. The camps placed a great emphasis on physical fitness and military training.

Even if the camp was ideal, boys and girls experienced fear and homesickness from being away from their families. Children as young as six were taken from their parents. Also, these Hitler Youths were evacuated from endangered cities and could not help but constantly wonder whether their families were alive and well after air raids and bombings. One KLV participant reflected on the effects of the fear, despair, and mourning that some students felt: "They probably only expressed themselves indirectly: the number of bedwetters was incredibly high and also we children were subject to strange outbursts which are difficult to explain but possibly derived from repressed anxiety states."[79]

It is also fairly certain that the education that boys and girls received in their particular camps placed more emphasis on physical fitness than their local schools had. Even though the camps were supposed to be run through a partnership of teachers and Hitler

Youth leaders, in reality the Hitler Youth had the greatest influence. This meant that an even greater emphasis was placed on physical fitness and military training in the camps and very little attention was paid to academic education. Proof of this can be seen in the fact that "test exercises were written collectively, with examinees freely copying from each other, while a trace of dust discovered in the course of a room inspection occasioned the most rigorous punishment."[80]

During the time that young people attended KLV camps, the Nazis were able to assume total control over their lives. These boys and girls had little contact with their parents except through letters, and even these were censored. The National Socialists achieved the same sort of influence in their elite boarding schools. In these schools, everything from meals to classes ran according to National Socialist ideology in an attempt to completely indoctrinate youngsters and own them.

The Complete Hitler Youth Experience

Resistance

When the Law Concerning the Hitler Youth passed in 1936 and the follow-up decree in 1939, every boy and girl of "pure German blood" was legally mandated to join the Hitler Youth organization. According to membership statistics, around two-thirds of German boys and girls were members before the passage of the law. The remaining third, well over 2 million young people, were now legally forced to become members. Not all were pleased about this state of affairs. Even so, very few youths resisted Nazi Germany. Forming resistance groups in the Third Reich was extremely difficult. Disagreeing with the Nazis was frequently seen as treason. Individuals who went so far as to oppose the Nazis had to work in secret to avoid putting themselves and their families at risk of being arrested, jailed, and killed. Karma Rauhut, who managed to avoid joining the BdM in the Third Reich, explains why she did not work against the Nazis:

> It was like you were in a spiderweb and the spider always noticed if something vibrated somewhere and did not ring true. . . . [People] said, "Ja, one could flee." *Where* should one flee to? You could only do resistance if you took death into consideration. Or horrible torture and also torture for your whole family, and death and KZ (concentration camp). And we are not all heroes. We shat our pants from fear. Not everyone is born to heroism.[81]

Two men suspected of treasonous activity are questioned by Nazi officials. Those who opposed the Third Reich risked being arrested, jailed, and killed.

Surrounded by a youth gang, a member of a Hitler Youth patrol receives a beating. Youth gangs also committed violent acts against pedestrians and uniformed officials.

Youth Gangs

Most young people did not openly defy the Nazis and small acts of dissent were the most common resistance to the Hitler Youth. A hostile group of gangs called the Edelweiss Pirates arose spontaneously in the late 1930s in Germany and was in some ways a response to the 1936 Hitler Youth law. Originally, they were local groups of boys and girls who remained outside the Hitler Youth. After 1939, however, many joined the Hitler Youth out of necessity and detested it. A 1944 report by the Reich Ministry of Justice described the appearance of the Edelweiss Pirates as well as how to recognize them in their Hitler Youth uniforms:

> They wear the Edelweiss badge on or under the left lapel or coloured pins in the colour of Edelweiss or in black, red and yellow. In so far as they belong to the HJ these badges are worn either openly or secretly on the uniform. One often sees the skull badge. The regulation uniform of the Edelweiss Pirates is short trousers, white socks, a check shirt, a white pullover and scarf and a windcheater. In addition, they have very long hair. A comb is worn in the left sock and a knife in the right one. In so far as girls belong to the gangs they wear white socks. A white pullover or waistcoat.[82]

Edelweiss Pirates were primarily found in cities, and most of them were working-class youths. They met in pubs and cafés to talk, sing, and hang out. They frequently listened to music that was frowned upon by the Nazis—popular songs from the United States or Great Britain. A favorite activity was to make up new lyrics for the Hitler Youth songs that they were forced to sing. On weekends they went on camping trips, hikes, and longer journeys to visit parts of Germany and Austria.

Not all Edelweiss Pirate activities were harmless. In Düsseldorf, the local authorities reported violent acts committed against pedestrians, and feces smeared in the faces of uniformed officials. Although activities such as these varied from gang to gang, the

The Reasons for Gang Activity

Gang activity in the Third Reich greatly troubled authorities. This can be seen in the 1944 report on "the emergence and combating of youth gangs" that was released by the Reich Ministry of Justice. The report contained a section that discussed what the authorities believed to be the reasons for this increase in activity. This portion of the report was taken from volume four of Jeremy Noakes's, *Nazism, 1919–1945: A Documentary Reader*.

"The appeal of the criminal/anti-social groups is primarily due to the fact, as has been mentioned already, that the war has resulted in a reduction in the supervision of young people who are especially liable to indulge in criminal acts and the fact that they are that much more exposed to infection from their environment.

The appeal of the politically hostile (i.e. Edelweiss Pirates) and liberal-individualistic (i.e. Swing Youth) groups has other causes in addition:

a) The young people who lack keenness are left to themselves a great deal. They avoid HJ duties as far as possible. . . . They meet in the streets or in the parks, bring along a musical instrument and soon form a group with each person making a contribution to its further development. It represents the urge to enjoy a group experience, something which can be regarded as a manifestation of puberty and which is not satisfied by the HJ. . . .

b) The urge to independence, which is naturally present in certain age groups, cannot be sensibly channeled by the parents, since the fathers are mostly away at the front and the mothers have either been conscripted for war work or are too weak firmly to oppose these activities. . . .

c) The deployment of young people in workplaces which they find uncongenial, in addition to the heavy demands being made upon them, produces signs of a lack of enthusiasm or tiredness, which leads to absenteeism."

dress of the Edelweiss Pirates and their hatred of Hitler Youth service united them. There was one other activity that banded Edelweiss Pirates together and made them problematic for the Nazis: their bashing of Hitler Youth patrols. When they spotted a patrol, whether they were on a weekend camping trip in the country or in the city, they first determined if they were strong enough to beat the patrol, and then they either fought them or avoided them.

The Edelweiss Pirates were primarily a rebellious group. They broke the rules that the Hitler Youth set for them through their extravagant dress, music choice, and Hitler Youth bashing—all behaviors that were con-

sidered unsuitable by Nazi standards. Few Edelweiss Pirates actually did anything to politically oppose the Nazis beyond this rebellious behavior. There were, however, a small number of Edelweiss Pirate members and even groups who worked against the Nazis, distributing Allied propaganda or working with other resistance groups such as the Communists to agitate against the Nazi regime.

The National Socialists considered the Edelweiss Pirates a significant threat and responded to them in kind. Some Edelweiss Pirates were caught by the gestapo or by the Hitler Youth secret police, a force that conducted raids and arrested youngsters. Pirates were warned, demoted in rank in the Hitler Youth, arrested, forced to go to weekend detention centers where they were fed only bread and water, and at times had their heads shaved so that everyone would know that they were considered traitors. Some gang leaders were sentenced to hard labor or imprisonment, but for the most part youth were caught and released with some sort of smaller punishment.

Swing Youth

The Swing Youth was another illegal youth group that arose in Nazi Germany. It got its name from the type of music that members listened to—swing music. This music came from England and the United States, where performers such as Glenn Miller, Benny Goodman, and Tommy Dorsey were popular.

Just as the Edelweiss Pirates were usually Hitler Youth members, so too were Swing Youth. However, whereas the Edelweiss Pirates tended to be from urban, working-class families, Swing Youth usually came from urban, middle-to-upper-class families. Their dress set them apart. They imitated English fashions and "often [wore] pleated jackets in tartan designs and [carried] umbrellas. As a badge they [wore] a colored dress-shirt button in the lapels."[83]

Swing Youth took every opportunity they could get to listen to swing and jazz music played either on records or by live bands. Originally, the Nazis allowed swing events to occur, but then Hitler Youth officials began to take offense and banned them. This forced the Swing Youth to meet, listen to music, and hold dances in secret. Secret swing clubs opened in many cities, and youth gathered there in the evenings and on weekends to dance the jitterbug or the rumba. Also, many swing kids held dances and parties for their group of friends at their homes when their parents were away.

The Swing Youth and the Edelweiss Pirates were open to both boys and girls, without separate divisions. This was very different from the Hitler Youth, in which boys and girls were not allowed to be part of the same group. Thus, it is not surprising that a great deal of dating and sexual exploration took place in both groups. The National Socialist officials took great offense at this. In the case of the Swing Youth, the Hitler Youth officials also disliked the fact that they allowed Jewish youth in their group and listened to music by African Americans.

Even though the Swing Youth was a rebellious group and only a few members worked to oppose the Nazis, the Nazi response to the swing kids was harsh. The leader of the SS, Heinrich Himmler, declared that all leaders of the Swing Youth, male or female, no matter what age, were to be sent to concentration camps. There, he ordered, they should be kept for two to three years. Their parents would also be investigated, and if they had known about or aided their children's actions, then they, too, should be sent to a concentration camp.

The White Rose

The White Rose was a group of young people who actively worked to bring about the downfall of the National Socialists. The group was founded by Hans Scholl, Jurgen Wittenstein, and Alexander Schmorell. They were joined by Christoph Probst, Willi Graf, and Hans's younger sister, Sophie Scholl. The original members of the White Rose were students at Munich University, and the group was supported by the university's philosophy professor, Kurt Huber, who wrote portions of their leaflets.

Both Hans and Sophie Scholl were at one time enthusiastic members of the Hitler Youth. Hans had even been a high-ranking leader. Their sister Inge Scholl explained the enthusiasm that she and her two siblings originally shared for the Hitler Youth organization:

> We loved our land dearly. . . . Our fatherland—what was it but the extended home of all those who shared a language and belonged to one people. . . . And Hitler . . . would help this fatherland to achieve greatness, fortune, and prosperity. He would see to it that everyone had work and bread. He would not rest until every German was independent, free, and happy in his fatherland. We found this good, and we were willing to do all we could to contribute to the common effort. But there was something else that drew us with mysterious power and swept us along: the closed ranks of marching youth with banners waving, eyes fixed straight ahead, keeping time to drumbeat and song. . . . It is not surprising that all of us, Hans and Sophie and the others, joined the Hitler Youth.[84]

However, after a series of events—not being allowed to sing songs he loved, fly the flag the boys in his unit had specially created, or read some of his favorite books—Hans Scholl became disgruntled with the organization. The rest of the Scholl children were also affected. They came to dislike the Hitler Youth as Hans's doubts spread to them and coincided with their learning of the existence of concentration camps and the disappearance of a favorite teacher. Hans and Sophie, once enthusiastic Hitler Youth leaders, went on to become members of the White Rose and to resist the Nazis.

The White Rose wrote, printed, and distributed leaflets that called for the overthrow of the Nazi government by the German people. The leaflets were written to reach German

The founders of the White Rose studied at the University of Munich (pictured). The leaflets they distributed were written in part by the university's philosophy professor.

Himmler's Response to Swing Youth

On January 26, 1942, Heinrich Himmler, the leader of the SS issued an order. He gave instructions on how the Hamburg Swing Youth were to be dealt with by the authorities. The order was translated by Peter D. Stachura and is included in his book *The German Youth Movement, 1900–1945.*

Heinrich Himmler took drastic measures against the Hamburg Swing Youth.

"I know that the Secret State Police has already taken action once. But it is now my opinion that the whole evil must be energetically eradicated. I am against taking half measures.

All ringleaders, male and female, as well as teachers who are dissident-minded and support the Swing Youth, are to be sent to concentration camps. There these youngsters must first of all be thrashed and then exercised and compelled to do hard labour. Any kind of work camp or youth detention camp is too mild for these fellows and useless girls. The girls are to be employed as weavers and agricultural workers during the summer.

They are to be kept in concentration camps for two to three years. It must be made clear that they can never again engage in study. The parents must be investigated to ascertain whether they supported their children. If they did, then they must also be confined in concentration camps and their property confiscated.

Only if we attack this problem in a brutal fashion can we avoid this dangerous anglophile tendency from spreading during a time when Germany is fighting for its existence."

citizens who did not want the Nazis in power but did nothing to stop them. This view was conveyed in the following passage from the group's third leaflet:

Our present "state" is the dictatorship of evil. "Oh, we've known that for a long time," I hear you object, "and it isn't necessary to bring that to our attention again." But, I ask you, if you know that, why do you not bestir yourselves, why do you allow these men who are in power to rob you step by step, openly and in secret, of one domain of your rights after another, until one day nothing, nothing at all will be left but a mechanized state system presided over by criminals and drunks?[85]

The White Rose asked people who believed that the Nazi state was wrong to begin passive resistance. It asked people to do their part, in whatever their line of work, to sabotage

The White Rose

The following is the fifth leaflet distributed by the White Rose resistance group. It is excerpted from the White Rose archive at http://members.aol.com/weiberose/index2.html.

"A Call to All Germans!

The war is approaching its destined end. As in the year 1918, the German government is trying to focus attention exclusively on the growing threat of submarine warfare, while in the East the armies are constantly in retreat and invasion is imminent in the West. Mobilization in the United States has not yet reached its climax, but already it exceeds anything that the world has ever seen. It has become a mathematical certainty that Hitler is leading the German people into the abyss. Hitler cannot win the war; he can only prolong it. The guilt of Hitler and his minions goes beyond all measure. Retribution comes closer and closer.

But what are the German people doing? They will not see and will not listen. Blindly they follow their seducers into ruin. Victory at any price! is inscribed on their banner. 'I will fight to the last man,' says Hitler—but in the meantime the war has already been lost.

Germans! Do you and your children want to suffer the same fate that befell the Jews? Do you want to be judged by the same standards as your traducers? Are we to be forever a nation which is hated and rejected by all mankind? No. Dissociate yourselves from National Socialist gangsterism. Prove by your deeds that you think otherwise. A new war of liberation is about to begin. The better part of the nation will fight on our side. Cast off the cloak of indifference you have wrapped around you. Make the decision before it is too late. Do not believe the National Socialist propaganda which has driven the fear of Bolshevism into your bones. Do not believe that Germany's welfare is linked to the victory of National Socialism for good or ill.

A criminal regime cannot achieve a German victory. Separate yourselves in time from everything connected with National Socialism. In the aftermath a terrible but just judgment will be meted out to those who stayed in hiding, who were cowardly and hesitant.

What can we learn from the outcome of this war—this war that never was a national war?

The imperialist ideology of force, from whatever side it comes, must be shattered for all time. A one sided Prussian militarism must never again be allowed to assume power. Only in large-scale cooperation among the nations of Europe can the ground be prepared for reconstruction. Centralized hegemony, such as the Prussian state has tried to exercise in Germany and in Europe, must be cut down at its inception. The Germany of the future must be a federal state. At this juncture only a sound federal system can imbue a weakened Europe with a new life. The workers must be liberated from their condition of down trodden slavery under National Socialism. The illusory structure of autonomous national industry must disappear. Every nation and each man have a right to the goods of the whole world!

Freedom of speech, freedom of religion, the protection of individual citizens from the arbitrary will of criminal regimes of violence—these will be the bases of the New Europe.

Support the resistance. Distribute the leaflets!"

Nazi efforts. It called on munitions workers to sabotage the war equipment they manufactured. All universities that helped the war effort through scientific discoveries or technical knowledge were to be undermined. People were not to participate in any cultural event that would make the National Socialists look good, and they were not to give money to any state organization, even seemingly humanitarian ones. The White Rose reasoned that if people passively refused to support the Nazi state, it would come to an end.

At first, group members only distributed these leaflets around the university; as time went on, they began to drop them in mailboxes around Munich. Eventually, they began to travel to other cities carrying suitcases full of leaflets to distribute. This was a dangerous undertaking, as Inge Scholl explains:

They had to stow their luggage in an inconspicuous place on the train; they had to get it past the numerous patrols of the army, the police, and even the Gestapo, who ran checks on the trains and sometimes inspected the luggage itself. . . . And how anxious you were if someone as much as looked at you. What fright when anyone came toward you—what relief when he passed by.[86]

Each member of the White Rose had his or her own job in the production and distribution of leaflets. Some wrote, and others worked on obtaining supplies and recruiting supporters. It was difficult to buy stamps in bulk without raising suspicion, so days were spent going from place to place purchasing stamps. Everyone assisted in the distribution of the leaflets. Some members of the White Rose even went beyond the leaflet work in their agitation for the downfall of the Nazis. On three separate nights, Hans Scholl, Schmorell, and Willi Graf wrote slogans such

Members of the White Rose distributed their leaflets by hand, dropped them in mailboxes, and posted them among other announcements on public message boards (pictured).

as "Down with Hitler" on the sides of houses in Munich. This was by far their most dangerous act since they could have been seen and arrested by Nazi patrols at any time.

Though all three young men survived these three dangerous nights, the White Rose was not so lucky a few days later when it began its next leaflet campaign. In the early morning of February 18, 1943, Hans and Sophie Scholl went to the university to distribute the sixth leaflet in lecture halls before classes began. Their actions were seen by a janitor who was a loyal Nazi Party member. All doors to the university were locked, the Scholls were trapped and arrested by the gestapo, and Christoph Probst was also arrested.

They were tried in the Nazi court which handed down the following decision:

> . . . The accused have in a time of war by means of leaflets called for the sabotage of the war effort and armaments and for the overthrow of the National Socialist way of life of our people, have propagated defeatist ideas, and have most vulgarly defamed the Führer, thereby giving aid to the enemy of the Reich and weakening the armed security of the nation.
>
> On this account they are to be punished by *Death*.[87]

Their death sentences were carried out in a matter of hours; a few weeks later, other members of the White Rose were also arrested. Professor Huber, Graf, and Schmorell were sentenced to death. Other peripheral participants received jail sentences anywhere from three months to life.

Other resistance groups opposed the Nazis during the Third Reich, most notably Communist and Socialist youths, however, the White Rose's activities and the Nazi response to them make it remarkable. Although the Nazis disapproved of the activities of the Edelweiss Pirates and the Swing Youth, few members worked in opposition to the regime, and they were more of a thorn in the Nazi side. As Germany continued to lose the war and more young people died, there was more dislike of the National Socialists and the Hitler Youth in general. As a result, there was more general youth resistance.

The Hitler Youth at War

When Germany went to war, the boys and girls of the Hitler Youth were prepared. They were a generation taught to worship and obey Hitler without question. Hitler youth, who were fed stories of heroes since childhood, were excited and willing to sacrifice themselves for Germany and the Aryan race. These young people wholeheartedly believed that the noble way to die, the only way to die, was for Hitler and Germany.

This devotion is illustrated in one American observer's story of a young *Pimpf* who contracted pneumonia. Although the boy was ill, his father and his Hitler Youth leader had forced him to participate in a multiple-day march. At the destination, he was promoted to the Jungvolk. The observer saw the boy once he was back home and very ill:

> From the cot came words—shrill, penetrating. "Let me die for Hitler. I *must* die for Hitler!" Over and over, pleading, accusing . . . fighting against life, fighting the doctor, fighting to die.

> "They told him at the [initiation] ceremony that he had to die for Hitler," the mother continued. . . . "His father says if he dies, then he dies for Hitler," the mother said tonelessly.[88]

The National Socialists exploited this sentiment, which they taught youngsters beginning at age six, when Germany went to war in 1939. If young people were willing to fight to die of pneumonia to achieve the glory of dying for Hitler, the Nazis knew they would be even more enthusiastic about dying in battle.

The Early Stages on the Home Front

Some Germans had always seen the paramilitary training of the Hitler Youth as a preparation for war. A group of German women who lived through the Third Reich were interviewed in the 1980s and asked if they had known the war was coming:

> Frau Amschel replied, "That we already knew, ne?" She said they saw the preparations for war. What kinds? "That they were in the club, ne? The Hitler club, that was all preparations, ne?" [Did she mean] the Hitler Youth was thought of as preparation for a war? They all agreed, at once.[89]

Although there is some argument as to whether the Hitler Youth organization was created to prepare youth for the war that Hitler began, there is very little dispute about the fact that the military training, physical fitness, and ideology of the group did prepare boys and girls for the war. Moreover, the boys in the special formations had extensive training in aeronautics, mechanics, and sailing. They were ready to be drafted into the military instead of merely the Nazi Party.

Three young members of the Hitler Youth watch as soldiers fire a machine gun during an exercise. The military training of the Hitler Youth was part of Germany's preparation for war.

In the first years of the war, the risks were relatively small. The Hitler Youth members were primarily active on the home front. Members of the Hitler Youth delivered men their call-up orders. Some boys worked as guides for troops stationed in their city, helped organize transports to assist civilians in leaving endangered areas, or dug trenches for troops. Both boys and girls picked plants and flowers for medicinal purposes. A great deal of the work done by members centered around obtaining food. They were asked to pick berries and collect various nuts and seeds. In 1942, 1.4 million girls and 600,000 boys assisted farmers in bringing in the harvest as part of their land service.

One large undertaking of Hitler Youth groups was the collection of materials deemed necessary for the war effort, such as metal and paper. They went door to door asking each family to give what they could. Oftentimes, this became a competition between different units to see who could collect the most. The youngsters were quite convincing. They sang, told jokes, and charmed many people into parting with their belongings. They were even able to convince families to part with items that were quite expensive, most notably skis, which were used during the winter on the Russian front.

Unique Tasks

Aside from participating in the collection of needed materials, Jungmädel and BdM girls also had some unique tasks to perform on the home front. The January 1940 issue of the official Nazi monthly journal explained some of the tasks that girls performed:

> The girls are no less committed [to the war effort] than the boys. In accordance with their female character and training they find employment in the auxiliary services of the Red Cross, assisting large

families and peasants' wives in the household; they look after children of working mothers, help with the distribution of ration cards, assist in kitchens and with the railway station service.[90]

All and all, the Hitler Youth members were very active in these early stages of the war. In the first months of the war, over 1 million boys and girls were deployed to various parts of Germany to assist on the home front. When they received their orders, they had to go. Even though all of these tasks were essential and fairly risk-free, as the war continued Hitler Youth members were asked to do tasks that were progressively more dangerous.

At the start of World War II over 7 million boys and girls were Hitler Youth members,

War Breaks Out

On September 1, 1939, World War II began when German troops attacked Poland. The following banner headline ran on the front page of the *New York Times* that day: "German Army Attacks Poland; Cities Bombed, Port Blockaded; Danzig Is Accepted into Reich." The paper included an article by Jerzy Szapiro titled simply, "Hostilities Begun." The article described the initial military actions that began World War II and cost the lives of millions.

"War began at 5 o'clock this morning with German planes attacking Gdynia, Cracow, and Katowice.

At Gdynia three bombs exploded in the sea.

The regular German Army started an offensive. . . .

At 9 o'clock an attempt was made to bombard Warsaw. The planes, however, did not reach even the suburbs. . . .

While this dispatch was being telephoned, the air-raid sirens sounded in Warsaw.

It was reported today that Tezew and Czestochowa were bombed by German airplanes early this morning.

There was no official confirmation of the bombing.

Fighting is reported at Danzig.

It was reported officially that German troops had attacked Polish defenses. . . . There was no announcement of the damage resulting from the bombing.

Mist and clouds were overhanging the city. A light drizzle apparently afforded momentary protection against air raids. Warsaw went to work as usual."

A German aircraft releases its bombs over Poland.

and many of them were willing to make any sacrifice for Hitler and Germany. The war had an immediate effect on the organization since many of its male leaders volunteered to serve in the German armed forces. These vacancies had to be filled, but in many cases not enough boys were eligible. As a result, the age that a boy must be to rise to a leadership position was lowered, and as the war progressed, lowered again. Alfons Heck—who was sixteen when he became a *Gefolgschaftsführer*—discussed his own rank in view of this general trend: "By [1944] it wasn't uncommon for a sixteen-year-old to head an *Unterbann* (four to six units numbering up to 800 members), but ours was a priority sector. I now commanded nearly 3,000."[91]

At the same time that the leadership of the Hitler Youth became younger and less experienced, the organization progressively militarized. In other words, boys who were less prepared were being asked to do more risky military tasks. This trend continued throughout the war and contributed to the high casualty rate among Hitler Youth members.

The Hitler Youth leadership reorganized in January 1941. At the time it had fourteen departments, which included everything from education to special formations. These departments were cut and tweaked to form three larger departments: military training, deployment, and ideological education. This reorganization was a symbol of the new role of the Hitler Youth in Germany. The military training department replaced the department of physical education in much the same way that military-related work had replaced sports and athletics in the organization.

Military Training

For boys, military training intensified. In 1942 basic training camps were created for boys over the age of sixteen and a half. These camps were intended to be a sort of crash course for young boys who, after completion, joined the army or the Luftwaffe. This somewhat prepared boys for their upcoming service in the military; however, as the war rolled

The collection of materials necessary for the war effort, such as metal (pictured), was an important undertaking of Hitler Youth groups.

War Is for Youth

Perhaps part of the reason why the Nazis were so willing to allow the Hitler Youth to participate to such a great degree in the war was their belief that youth would always triumph over age. The *Schwarze Korps*, a publication for the members of the SS, contained the following article that gave the youth of German troops and their leader, Hitler, as a primary reason for victory. This excerpt was translated and appeared in the U.S. publication the *Living Age* in August 1940.

"The spirit of the victor must be young. And our troops are young, and young are the methods of our attack. . . . Who among the octogenarians (80 year olds) of the enemy would have believed, a few months ago, that the gigantic works of the Maginot Line could be stormed successfully by individual acts of manliness?

But our youth is not only young in years. Motivating it is the youthful vigor of our revolutionary ideal. . . .

In this [day]—as in every era of history—one law has invariably proved its unchanging truth: youth will always triumph over age.

The old nations must disappear when their hour strikes. Who can reasonably expect any other outcome at this time when one nation, become conscious of the power of its youth, sees in another merely a [group] of quarrelsome old men who have lost faith even in their own people? To express it another way, the secret of our military victories lies in our conquest over the symptoms of age. . . .

The German people had to suffer the most humiliating downfall to arrive at a point where they could discard the old, the obsolete and obstructive. We had to change from the bottom up; a new and youthful spirit, in a totalitarian sense, had to dominate our thinking and our actions in every field. From the depths of the soul of our people emerged an enlightened and purified understanding of the meaning of German life and of Germany's struggle. And again from those depths of the German people there came forward a Leader of the young of Germany, and of her young soldiers, the symbol in himself of our victory over ourselves and the guarantor of eventual victory over our enemies."

on and Germany needed more soldiers, even this small bit of preparatory training was reduced. The result was boys in uniform who were very young and wholly unprepared for war but who dreamed of being heroes—dying for Hitler.

In 1943 things became riskier for Hitler Youths when boys in the HJ who were over fifteen were called up mainly to man antiaircraft gunnery units. Because of the need for manpower, younger boys were also involved. The older boys worked the guns, and younger members used the searchlight or carried messages. Karl Damm recalled that in 1943, just before his sixteenth birthday, his military involvement began:

> I reported, like almost all of my classmates, to the 2nd battery of the 267th Heavy Anti-Aircraft Battalion for service in the flak auxiliary.

> Service in the flak auxiliary had many fascinating aspects. In the first place, we were impressed by the fact that we were now soldiers. Then there were our guns, the heavy

In this poster, a member of the Hitler Youth is ready to help fight fires caused by air raids. Older boys in the HJ manned antiaircraft guns.

8.8cm and the light 2cm guns. Finally, we were intrigued by the technology.[92]

During air raids, these battalions of young boys—and later girls—attempted to shoot down enemy aircraft. Afterward, Hitler Youth members organized to assist families who had either been hurt or had lost their homes in the bombings. In the midst of all this chaos, boys and girls were expected to continue their schooling. One former Hitler Youth recalled that "as incredible as it sounds, our regular school teachers came out to our firing positions and held 22 hours of classroom instruction a week, literally between the guns."[93]

Eventually, schools throughout Germany were closed due to the war.

Panzer Division Hitlerjungend

Also in 1943, a special division of the combat wing of the SS was created specifically for Hitler Youths: the Twelfth SS-Panzer Division Hitlerjungend. Many of the boys recruited to serve in this special tank division were under the age of sixteen as they set out to war. There was a great deal of tragic irony in the situation: The National Socialists had passed laws to "protect youth" that forbade young people under sixteen from drinking or smoking, but they asked them to go into battle relatively unprepared and to die for Germany.

Whereas some of the boys enthusiastically volunteered to be part of the Twelfth SS-Panzer Division, one man remembered how HJ members were forced to join in his district:

All the HJ Home Guard [Volkssturm] members were assembled in a common room which was then locked and a guard placed outside! Our HJ district leader made a speech in the presence of the instructors. He declared that, according to a secret order from the Führer, all offers to volunteer for active service were no longer valid except for those for the SS and for the one-man torpedo weapons. He therefore called on those present to volunteer for the SS en masse; it was, he said, a matter of honour to do so. But if this did not occur "he had plenty of time." The room would remain locked until evening; there would be no meals and anyone who did not sign up for the SS would be sent straight to a "recruitment camp."[94]

War Efforts of Hitler Youths

The National Socialists used young people extensively in their war effort. Karl O. Paetel, a U.S. journalist, wrote about this unprecedented practice in the April 1, 1944, edition of the *Nation*.

"According to the Nazi press, 362 boys and girls in the Seventh district of Berlin were taken into the National Socialist Party in the middle of 1943; 162 of them were already in the army. Assuming that about half the total number were girls, it appears that all the seventeen-year-old boys in the district had volunteered (a boy of seventeen may join the army either as a private or as a long-term officer candidate). Lately more and more sixteen-year-olds have been appearing at the front, and it is reported that fifteen-year-olds are now permitted to volunteer.

Many schoolboys are drafted into the Luftwaffe (air force) or the navy as "helpers." They live in barracks or on ships, under the supervision of a Hitlerjungend leader who acts as foreman. Those who want to join the Waffen-SS may notify the Labor Service at the age of sixteen and a half, and with its permission may transfer to the S.S. after half a year, or even three months. Time spent in the Black Shirts (S.S.) is credited to their Labor Service records.

On May 5, 1942, a decree issued jointly by the president of the National Socialist Teachers' League and the Man-Power Commissioner authorized the employment of boys and girls as helpers in a variety of occupations. Some 250,000 members of the Hitlerjungend have since joined fire brigades; more than a million members of the Bund deutscher Mädchen are in the Sanitation, Health, and Household Help Service; the Deutsches Jungvolk has long been assigning its members to salvage and farm service; the Hitlerjungend and the Jungmädel likewise enlist their members in the scrap-metal service, and such other jobs as helping in railroad stations and caring for workers' children. At the beginning of this year plans were under way for the organization of a courier service using boys ten to thirteen years old and of 'flying squadrons' of sixteen-year-olds to help the police and the Waffen-S.S., with full police powers. Many boys and girls thirteen to fifteen years old work in war industries. With iron consistency the Nazi Party has organized the life of German youth for its own purposes. The individual lives of these young people are being swallowed up in the common life of the organizations to which they belong."

One of the 250,000 Hitlerjugend who joined fire brigades during the war.

Volunteers or not, the members of the Twelfth SS-Panzer Division saw their first action at the Battle of Normandy. Its commanding officer, Kurt Meyer, remarked later that "this division displayed against discouraging odds a fanatical courage which was acknowledged by even its bitterest enemies."[95] Some "enemies" did indeed remark about the fanatical determination of the division. It was the Allied forces first run-in with the Hitler Youth, a generation educated since childhood to hate them, to fight or die, and to believe that the future of humankind depended on their sacrifice. One Allied doctor encountered this attitude in a young boy with multiple shrapnel wounds: "He was about 14, and looked like he was in a trance. I leaned over him and said in German, 'You dummy! Look at what this has gotten you!' Well, that boy suddenly heaved himself up, spat in my face, and shouted, 'Long live the Führer!'"[96]

After some initial success at Normandy, the division suffered heavy casualties: "Within a month the *Hitlerjungend* Division had lost 20% of men killed, 40% missing and wounded, and 50% of its tanks and armored vehicles."[97]

In late 1944 German war losses reached such a height that the Volkssturm was created. The Volkssturm was a home guard in which every man age sixteen to sixty had to participate. Boys became part of tank destroyer troops within the Volkssturm. These troops and their actions were described by Gerhard Rempel in his book *Hitler's Children: The Hitler Youth and the SS*:

> The actual combat unit, or Troop, consisted of nine boys, two groups of three manning *Panzerfausts* (bazookas) and the remaining three carrying machine guns for protection. . . . On the company level, three-quarters of the boys were to erect tank traps and one-quarter were to be engaged in destroying tanks with bazookas.[98]

At times the boys—and girls, beginning in the spring of 1945—who were shooting at enemy tanks were actually much younger than sixteen. Hugo Stehkämper, who was drafted into the Volkssturm at fifteen, remembers "an eight-year-old . . . who had destroyed a tank with a bazooka."[99]

In the Volkssturm, boys and girls were also killed in great numbers. An HJ leader, Günter Fraschka, gave an account of his war experience:

> I saw . . . how . . . youth was driven to the front and sacrificed in the fire storm. . . . The boys who fell beside me were fourteen and fifteen years old. . . . I led a combat group that was made up almost exclusively of children. I am one of the few who survived. The others perished, died in atrocious agony.[100]

As Germany lost more men, younger and younger boys and girls were called on to fill their vacant positions. Boys who dreamed of winning medals for bravery and honor, of winning the war for Germany, were now faced with the brutal realities of actual war. One BdM leader recalled,

> In one suburb of Berlin I saw a row of dead anti-aircraft auxiliaries lying side by side. It was just after an air raid. The anti-aircraft base where these schoolboys were serving had received several direct hits. I went into a barrack room where the survivors were gathered. They sat on the floor along one wall, and the white faces they turned towards me were distorted with fear. Many of them were weeping.[101]

Hitler meets with older members of the HJ who have been injured in the war. During his final days, Hitler was defended by children.

Imagining a heroic war, they were not prepared for having friends lose their lives, being wounded, killing others, or dying themselves. Some tried to run away and were executed for desertion. Some were scared, others hardened. Few actually knew how to fight in a battle since they had received very little training. This resulted in many casualties. The fact that some Hitler Youth members were so willing to die for Hitler, to fight or die, also caused many casualties since units fought to the last man, refusing to surrender even when faced with great odds.

During his final days in Berlin, Hitler was defended by children; although the war was lost, he still tried to inspire them to victory, to sacrifice their young lives. A newspaper report from the time describes an incident where the führer received twenty members of the Hitler Youth in his headquarters:

> The youngest of the retinue who were lined up was the 12-year-old Hitler Youth Alfred Czech, who rescued twelve wounded soldiers under enemy artillery and machine-gun fire. . . . Some of the 15-, 16- and 17-year-old boys were surrounded for days on end. They all assisted the troops and the Home Guard wherever they could. . . .

> The Führer greeted each of the Hitler boys with a handshake and listened to the accounts of their experiences. Finally, the Führer declared: ". . . Despite all the difficulties which currently face us, I am convinced that we shall be victorious in the struggle above all because of German youth and, in particular, because of you, my boys." [102]

In the end, it was the Hitler Youth who guarded Hitler's bunker, willing to fight to the death to protect him from the tanks that rolled into Berlin on April 30, 1945. In the so-called Battle of Berlin, "a total of 5,000 Hitler Youths were involved. . . . A mere 500 survived." [103] As these young people who were educated to be loyal Nazis and to sacrifice their lives for the cause fought outside, inside this bunker Hitler committed suicide, leaving his youth, or what was left of it after casualties, to deal with the aftermath of the war.

Life After Hitler and the Third Reich

Young people who were raised to worship Hitler, who were indoctrinated from age six to believe and embody Nazi ideology, were left with a defeated Germany and a dead führer. The Hitler Youth organization had reached into and shaped every aspect of their lives from schooling to their relations with family and friends. Suddenly, it was gone.

Not only was the organization gone, but the National Socialists were also hated by the world, including many Germans. The atrocities committed during the Third Reich, especially the Holocaust, came to the forefront. Some Hitler Youths were horrified by the camps and the Nazi role in them. In general, Hitler Youth members had a difficult time reconciling themselves with a führerless, defeated Germany and the Holocaust. However, they were young and had a great deal of their lives left to live.

Some returned to school. There, the number of young people who died in the war was highlighted when only a third to a half of some classes returned. Theo Loch, a former Hitler Youth and Luftwaffe member, remembered that only thirteen of his thirty-two classmates returned. This, combined with older party members not claiming any responsibility for Nazi Germany, insisting that "they never knew anything" caused his break from Nazi ideology. He recalls, "That was when I truly recognized how grossly betrayed we had actually been. A generation had been raised to die—to pass the big test—and then it was betrayed."[104]

This sense of betrayal is a common theme among the writings of former Hitler Youth members. Some felt that their desire to do well was utilized to help the National Socialists commit atrocities such as the Holocaust. Although some had a sense of what was going on in the concentration camps—some observers even argue that there was no way that other Germans could not have known—they contend that it was difficult to comprehend, especially as children. Karma Rauhut discussed this phenomenon:

"A friend of my father's came to our house and told us he had seen, in Poland, an entire airplane hangar full of corpses." A long pause followed.

Such information just does not "fit in your head," [Rauhut] later said. "Can you picture a whole airplane hangar full of corpses if you haven't seen them? It surpasses one's power of imagination. This inhuman criminality surpassed every power of imagination."[105]

However, after the defeat of Germany, young Germans no longer had to imagine, they could see with their own eyes. Some began to realize that the ideology they had been taught was not true. Images of the survivors of concentration camps and their stories greatly affected many. Throughout the war the Nazis told the Hitler Youth that the Allies would exterminate the German people if they won the

For many former members of the Hitler Youth, coming to terms with their role in Nazi Germany was a slow and painful process.

war. This was not happening in the war's aftermath, and some members realized that it was instead the Nazis who had been doing the exterminating. Some Hitler Youths, called Werewolves, continued to resist the Allies, but for the most part the war ended with Hitler's death. Some Hitler Youths held onto portions of Nazi ideology, but others began the slow and painful process of coming to terms with their role in Nazi Germany. They began de-Nazification and became citizens of a new Germany that was not ruled by National Socialists.

Today many former Hitler Youth members are successful adults. Some no longer believe the National Socialist ideology of their youth, but others do. Some former Hitler Youths write and speak to children about their experiences and try to help bring about a better understanding of Nazi Germany. They hope that an understanding of what happened will keep future generations from propagating hate and repeating the history of the Third Reich.

Notes

Chapter 1: Joining the Hitler Youth

1. Alfons Heck, *The Burden of Hitler's Legacy*. Frederick, CO: Renaissance House, 1988, p. 88.

2. Claudia Koonz, *Mothers in the Fatherland: Women, the Family, and Nazi Politics*. New York: St. Martin's, 1987, p. 150.

3. Quoted in Peter D. Stachura, *The German Youth Movement, 1900–1945: An Interpretative and Documentary History*. New York: St. Martin's, 1981, pp. 179–80.

4. Quoted in Roselle Chartock and Jack Spencer, eds., *The Holocaust Years: Society on Trial*. New York: Bantam Books, 1978, p. 122.

5. Baldur von Schirach, *Die Hitler Jungend: Idee und Gestalt*. Leipzig: Roehler & Umelang, 1934, p. 130.

6. Heck, *The Burden of Hitler's Legacy*, p. 57.

7. Quoted in Norman H. Baynes, ed., *The Speeches of Adolf Hitler: April 1922–August 1939*, vol. 1. London: Oxford University Press, 1942, pp. 541–42.

8. Melita Maschmann, *Account Rendered: A Dossier on My Former Self*. London: Abelyard-Schuman, 1965, p. 12.

9. Quoted in Heck, *The Burden of Hitler's Legacy*, p. 58.

10. Maschmann, *Account Rendered*, p. 12.

11. Quoted in Erika Mann, *School for Barbarians: Education Under the Nazis*. New York: Modern Age, 1938, p. 29.

12. Quoted in Baynes, *The Speeches of Adolf Hitler*, p. 538.

13. Heck, *The Burden of Hitler's Legacy*, p. 56.

14. Quoted in Baynes, *The Speeches of Adolf Hitler*, p. 546.

15. International Military Tribunal, *Trial of the Major War Criminals Before the International Military Tribunal*, vol. 14. Nuremberg: International Military Tribunal, 1948, p. 376.

16. Quoted in H. W. Koch, *The Hitler Youth: Origins and Development, 1922–45*. New York: Stein and Day, 1976, p. 100.

17. Quoted in Jeremy Noakes and Geoffrey Pridham, eds., *Nazism, 1919–1945: A Documentary Reader*, vol. 2, *State, Economy, and Society*. Exeter, Devon, UK: University of Exeter Press, 1995. p. 418.

18. Heck, *The Burden of Hitler's Legacy*, p. 57.

19. Koch, *The Hitler Youth*, p. 113.

20. Gregor Ziemer, *Education for Death: The Making of the Nazi*. London: Oxford University Press, 1941, p. 83.

21. Ziemer, *Education for Death*, p. 123.

Chapter 2: The Race War

22. Douglas J. Futuyma, *Evolutionary Biology*, Sinauer Associates, 1986. www. talkorigins.org/faqs/evolution-definition.html.

23. Laurence Moran, "What Is Evolution?" January 1993. www.talkorigins.org/faqs/evolution-definition.html.

24. Adolf Hitler, *Mein Kampf.* New York: Reynal & Hitchcock, 1939, p. 397.

25. Quoted in George L. Mosse, *Nazi Culture: Intellectual, Cultural, and Social Life in the Third Reich.* New York: Grosset & Dunlap, 1966, p. 62.

26. Hitler, *Mein Kampf*, p. 397.

27. Harwood L. Childs, trans., *The Nazi Primer: Official Handbook for Schooling the Hitler Youth.* New York: Harper & Brothers, 1938, p. 20.

28. Hitler, *Mein Kampf*, p. 581.

29. Quoted in Noakes and Pridham, *Nazism, 1919–1945*, vol. 2, p. 449.

30. Koonz, *Mothers in the Fatherland*, p. 197.

31. Quoted in Alison Owings, *Frauen: German Women Recall the Third Reich.* New Brunswick, NJ: Rutgers University Press, 1993, p. 346.

32. Maschmann, *Account Rendered*, p. 121.

Chapter 3: Ideology and Activities

33. Quoted in Richard Grunberger, *A Social History of the Third Reich.* London: Weidenfeld and Nicolson, 1971, p. 271.

34. Childs, *The Nazi Primer*, pp. 77–78.

35. Quoted in Owings, *Frauen*, p. 174.

36. Solomon Perel, *Europa, Europa.* New York: John Wiley & Sons, 1997, p. 133.

37. Childs, *The Nazi Primer*, p. 105.

38. Hitler, *Mein Kampf*, p. 613.

39. Quoted in Baynes, *The Speeches of Adolf Hitler*, p. 547.

Chapter 4: The School Day of the Hitler Youth

40. Quoted in Joachim von Ribbentrop, ed., *Germany Speaks.* London: Thornton Butterworth, 1938, p. 102.

41. Quoted in von Ribbentrop, *Germany Speaks*, p. 100.

42. Quoted in *Education in Nazi Germany.* London: Kulturkampf Association, 1938, p. 17.

43. Quoted in Owings, *Frauen*, p. 220.

44. Ilse McKee, *Tomorrow the World.* London: J. M. Dent & Sons, 1960, pp. 11–12.

45. Ziemer, *Education for Death*, pp. 67–68.

46. Frederic Sondern Jr., "Thousand-Year Reich," *Reader's Digest*, September 1939, p. 50.

47. Gilmer W. Blackburn, *Education in the Third Reich: Race and History in Nazi Textbooks.* Albany: State University of New York Press, 1985, p. 42.

48. Quoted in *Education in Nazi Germany*, p. 43.

49. Quoted in Mann, *School for Barbarians*, p. 68.

50. Quoted in von Ribbentrop, *Germany Speaks*, pp. 111–12.

51. Hitler, *Mein Kampf*, p. 616.

52. Quoted in Ziemer, *Education for Death*, p. 66.

53. Quoted in *Education in Nazi Germany*, p. 16.

54. Ziemer, *Education for Death*, p. 132.

Chapter 5: Home Life

55. Quoted in Owings, *Frauen*, p. 243.

56. Quoted in Lisa Pine, *Nazi Family Policy, 1933–1945.* Oxford: Berg, 1997, pp. 57–58.

57. Quoted in Perel, *Europa, Europa*, p. 118.

58. Grunberger, *A Social History of the Third Reich*, p. 240.

59. Grunberger, *A Social History of the Third Reich*, p. 242.

60. Heck, *The Burden of Hitler's Legacy*, p. 83.

61. Quoted in Stachura, *The German Youth Movement, 1900–1945*, p. 178.

62. Koch, *The Hitler Youth*, p. 109.

63. Quoted in Jeremy Noakes, *Nazism, 1919–1945: A Documentary Reader*, vol. 4, *The German Home Front in World War II*. Exeter, Devon, England: Exeter University Press, 1998, p. 112.

64. Quoted in Mosse, *Nazi Culture*, p. 241.

65. Stachura, *The German Youth Movement, 1900–1945*, p. 92.

66. Koch, *The Hitler Youth*, p. 121.

67. Maschmann, *Account Rendered*, p. 150.

68. Quoted in Grunberger, *A Social History of the Third Reich*, p. 273.

Chapter 6: The Complete Hitler Youth Experience

69. Koch, *The Hitler Youth*, p. 185.

70. Sondern, "Thousand-Year Reich," p. 53.

71. Quoted in Grunberger, *A Social History of the Third Reich*, p. 298.

72. Quoted in Noakes, *Nazism, 1919–1945*, vol. 4, p. 423.

73. Stachura, *The German Youth Movement, 1900–1945*, p. 156.

74. Jost Hermand, *A Hitler Youth in Poland: The Nazis' Program for Evacuating Children During World War II*. Evanston, IL: Northwestern University Press, 1997, p. 31.

75. Quoted in Noakes, *Nazism, 1919–1945*, vol. 4, p. 438.

76. Quoted in Noakes, *Nazism, 1919–1945*, vol. 4, p. 438.

77. Hermand, *A Hitler Youth in Poland*, p. 50.

78. Quoted in Noakes, *Nazism, 1919–1945*, vol. 4, p. 439.

79. Quoted in Noakes, *Nazism, 1919–1945*, vol. 4, p. 439.

80. Grunberger, *A Social History of the Third Reich*, p. 301.

Chapter 7: Resistance

81. Quoted in Owings, *Frauen*, p. 349.

82. Quoted in Noakes, *Nazism, 1919–1945*, vol. 4, p. 452.

83. Quoted in Noakes, *Nazism, 1919–1945*, vol. 4, p. 453.

84. Inge Scholl, *The White Rose: Munich, 1942–1943*. Middletown, CT: Wesleyan University Press, 1983, p. 6.

85. White Rose Archive, third leaflet of the White Rose. http://members.aol.com/weiberose.

86. Scholl, *The White Rose*, p. 44.

87. Scholl, *The White Rose*, p. 114.

Chapter 8: The Hitler Youth at War

88. Ziemer, *Education for Death*, pp. 80–81.

89. Quoted in Owings, *Frauen*, p. 236.

90. Quoted in Noakes, *Nazism, 1919–1945*, vol. 4, p. 399.

91. Heck, *The Burden of Hitler's Legacy*, p. 108.

92. Quoted in Johannes Steinhoff, Peter Pechel, and Dennis Showalter, eds., *Voices from the Third Reich: An Oral History*. Washington, DC: Regnery Gateway, 1989, p. 475.

93. Quoted in Steinhoff, Pechel, and Showalter, *Voices from the Third Reich*, p. 488.

94. Quoted in Noakes, *Nazism, 1919–1945*, vol. 4, p. 413.

95. Quoted in Stachura, *The German Youth Movement, 1900–1945*, pp. 164–65.

96. Quoted in Steinhoff, Pechel, and Showalter, *Voices from the Third Reich*, p. 426.

97. Koch, *The Hitler Youth*, p. 247.

98. Gerhard Rempel, *Hitler's Children: The Hitler Youth and the SS*. Chapel Hill: University of North Carolina Press, 1989, p. 238.

99. Quoted in Steinhoff, Pechel, and Showalter, *Voices from the Third Reich*, p. 491.

100. Quoted in Rempel, *Hitler's Children*, p. 243.

101. Maschmann, *Account Rendered*, p. 157.

102. Quoted in Noakes, *Nazism, 1919–1945*, vol. 4, pp. 414–15.

103. Rempel, *Hitler's Children*, p. 242.

Conclusion: Life After Hitler and the Third Reich

104. Quoted in Steinhoff, Pechel, and Showalter, *Voices from the Third Reich*, p. 495.

105. Quoted in Owings, *Frauen*, p. 353.

Glossary

Adolf Hitler Schools: Elite boarding schools in Nazi Germany that were created and run by the National Socialist Party.

Air HJ: An elite HJ formation in which boys could receive special training about aviation.

anti-Semitism: Hostility toward ethnic and/or religious Jewish people.

Aryan race: The Nazis believed this was the race of culture founders. They described Aryans as being blond-haired, blue-eyed, tall, and slender and having rosy white skin with a high-set nose and a small face; also referred to as the Nordic race.

biological evolution: A process that results in hereditary changes in a population spread over many generations.

black market: Trading goods without governmental permission.

blood-mixing: The Nazis believed this occurred when two people from different races had sexual relations.

Bund deutscher Mädel (BdM): A Hitler Youth group for girls fourteen to eighteen.

concordat: An agreement between the pope and a secular government.

culture destroyers: The Nazis believed that these were races of people who set back civilization; the Jewish people were thought to be culture destroyers.

culture founders: The Nazis believed that these were races of people who made advances in technology, art, etc., that result in human progress; the Aryan race was thought to be culture founders.

curriculum: The concepts and ideas covered by a teacher and students in a class.

dictatorship: A form of government in which one leader makes all of the decisions for the country.

Edelweiss Pirates: Youth gangs primarily made up of urban, working-class youth who spent their free time together and attacked Hitler Youth patrols.

Equestrian HJ: An elite HJ formation in which boys learned about riding and caring for horses.

eugenics: A pseudoscience that was founded in the late nineteenth century by Francis Galton. Eugenics attempted to improve the "breed" of human beings through planned marriage and reproduction.

Faith and Beauty: A Hitler Youth group for girls eighteen to twenty-one.

fit: A eugenic term for people who exhibit only favorable traits.

führer: The German word for leader. The Nazis called their leader, Adolf Hitler, the führer.

gestapo: The secret state police in the Third Reich. It was dedicated to maintaining the Nazi regime by tracking down and eliminating all dissidents, complainers, and opponents of the National Socialists.

Gleichschaltung: The coordination of German society. Once in power, the National

Socialists banned opposition groups in every facet of German society so that all actions and deeds would fit with the Nazi worldview.

Heimabende: Evening classes in which Hitler Youth members received instruction about National Socialist ideology.

hereditary disease: Disease passed from parent to child genetically.

Hitler Youth organization: The official youth group of the National Socialist German Workers' Party, includes all formations of boys and girls.

Hitler Youth secret police: An elite HJ formation that acted as the internal police of the Hitler Youth. It was used to infiltrate opposition groups and keep Hitler Youths in line.

Hitlerjungend (HJ): Hitler Youth formations for boys fourteen to eighteen.

Holocaust: The planned, systematic extermination of groups of people, including Jews, Gypsies, Russians, homosexuals, people with disabilities, Jehovah's Witnesses, Polish people, and people deemed politically unreliable, in concentration camps in Nazi Germany.

Jungmädel: A Hitler Youth group for girls ten to fourteen.

Jungvolk: The Hitler Youth formation for boys ages ten to fourteen.

Kinderlandverschickung (KLV) program: Originally a program to send urban Hitler Youth members who became ill to the country to recuperate; during the war it became a program to evacuate children from endangered areas.

Kristallnacht (Crystal Night): A Jewish pogrom that occurred on November 9, 1938; also called the Night of Broken Glass.

land service: A service that the Hitler Youth suggested every member perform. They usually helped farmers bring in the harvest or assisted families with many children.

Law Against Overcrowding of German Schools and Universities: A 1933 law that set a quota on the number of Jewish students that a school could have.

Law Concerning the Hitler Youth: A 1936 law that made membership in the Hitler Youth mandatory for all eligible boys and girls.

Law for the Protection of German Blood and Honor: A 1935 law that forbade marriage and sexual relations between Aryans and people of Jewish descent.

Law for the Protection of Hereditary Health: A 1933 law that called for the sterilization of people with hereditary illnesses.

Law for the Protection of Youth: A 1940 law that banned people under eighteen from restaurants, cinemas, and the streets after dark and those under sixteen from smoking or drinking in public.

leadership principle: The concept on which Nazi society was organized. Orders originate with the dictator (Hitler), and every individual must obey his superior without question so that Hitler's orders are systematically carried down through society.

lebensraum: Living space for the *Volk*.

Motor HJ: An elite HJ formation in which boys learned about driving and mechanics.

nationalism: A citizen's dedication to the interests of his or her own nation.

National Political Education Institutions (Napolas): Elite boarding schools in Nazi

Germany. They were similar to military schools and were run by the state.

natural selection: An aspect of Darwin's theory of evolution; the process that results in the survival of only those organisms that have favorable variations.

Naval HJ: An elite HJ formation in which boys learned about sailing.

Nazi: A member of the National Socialist German Workers' Party.

negative eugenics: Eugenic measures that work to decrease the population that is seen as unfit.

Nordic race: Another name for the Aryan race.

Ordensburgen: Finishing schools for the top Adolf Hitler School alumni.

pedagogy: The way a teacher teaches.

Pimpf: A member of the Jungvolk.

pogroms: Organized massacres.

positive eugenics: Eugenic measures that work to increase the population that is seen as fit.

propaganda: Information that is carefully presented and spread to promote a cause.

race: The Nazis believed a race of human beings was a group that distinguished itself by a combination of physical and spiritual characteristics and reproduced itself.

race war: The war that the Nazis believed was taking place between the Aryan culture founders and the Jewish culture destroyers.

racially pure: The Nazi ideal, an Aryan who is free of hereditary disease.

Reichstag: The German congress.

SA: Nazi Party members called storm troopers who took over some police duties during the Third Reich.

SS: The elite guard of the Nazi Party, also known as the Black Order because of the black shirts they wore. Used as political police in the Third Reich. Administered the concentration camps.

separate spheres: In Nazi society men and women had very different roles. Each was said to have its own separate sphere of influence.

social Darwinism: The application of Darwin's theory of biological evolution to societies.

Socialism: A political ideology in which the community owns all businesses, land, and money.

survival of the fittest: An aspect of Darwin's theory of evolution; refers to the fact that in the process of natural selection different variations of species struggle for existence, and the variation best equipped to live in the environment survives.

Swing Youth: Predominantly middle- to upper-class boys and girls who listened to swing and jazz music of which the Nazis did not approve.

theory: A proposed explanation or way of thinking about something.

Third Reich: Another term for Nazi Germany; Germany between the years of 1933 and 1945.

unfit: A eugenic term for people who have unfavorable traits.

variation: An aspect of Darwin's theory of evolution; it refers to the fact that organisms spontaneously change from one generation to the next.

Volk: The Nazi term for people who were considered of "pure German blood" or members of the German race.

Volk **community:** All people of German blood around the world.

Volkssturm: A home guard created toward the end of the war. Every man sixteen to sixty had to join this guard.

weltanschauung: German word for "world-view" or "ideology."

White Rose: A resistance group that distributed pamphlets calling for the downfall of the Nazis through the passive resistance of Germans. The group was caught, and its members were sentenced to death.

For Further Reading

Books

Eleanor H. Ayer, with Helen Waterford and Alfons Heck, *Parallel Journeys*. New York: Atheneum Books for Young Readers, 1995. This book alternates chapters between Waterford, who was in a concentration camp, and Heck, who became a high-ranking member of the Hitler Youth. It provides a wonderful contrast between the experiences of these two youths during the Third Reich.

Christabel Bielenberg, *Christabel Bielenberg and Nazi Germany*. Ed. Jane Shuter. Austin, TX: Raintree Steck-Vaughn, 1996. This book does a good job explaining the conditions in Nazi Germany. Excerpts from the perspective of an upper-middle-class woman.

Roselle Chartock and Jack Spencer, eds., *The Holocaust Years: Society on Trial*. New York: Bantam Books, 1978. Contains a variety of primary documents and first-person accounts of Nazi Germany. Includes pieces such as "Why I Joined the Hitler Youth" as well as primary documents on Nazi ideology, euthanasia, and the Holocaust.

Alexa Dvorson, *The Hitler Youth: Marching Toward Madness*. New York: Rosen, 1999. The biographical story of one German boy who willingly joined the Hitler Youth.

Elsbeth Emmerich, *My Childhood in Nazi Germany*. East Sussex, England: Wayland, 1991. Emmerich (born in 1934) describes her experiences growing up in Nazi Germany. This is a fairly good first-hand account since Emmerich—only eleven at the end of the Third Reich—also relies on facts from her family and quotes from her father's letters to complete her account.

Charles Hannam, *A Boy in That Situation: An Autobiography*. New York: Harper & Row, 1978. Hannam's autobiography describes his childhood years in Nazi Germany and his later years in England.

Eileen Heyes, *Children of the Swastika: The Hitler Youth*. Brookfield, CT: Millbrook, 1993. A good historical account of the history of the Hitler Youth movement and its ideology, including a discussion of World War II and the significant role that the organization played in it.

Ilse Koehn, *Mischling, Second Degree: My Childhood in Nazi Germany*. New York: Greenwillow Books, 1977. These are the memoirs of Ilse Koehn, who, as a girl in Nazi Germany, became a leader among the Hitler Youth. She did this as her Social Democratic family kept from her the secret of her partial Jewish heritage.

Solomon Perel, *Europa, Europa*. New York: John Wiley & Sons, 1997. The memoirs of Perel, who, as a Jewish child in Nazi Germany, hid in the Hitler Youth and became a leader.

Richard Procktor, *Nazi Germany: The Origins and Collapse of the Third Reich*. New York: Holt, Rinehart, and Winston, 1970. A general political history of Nazi Germany.

Inge Scholl, *The White Rose: Munich, 1942–1943*. Middletown, CT: Wesleyan University Press, 1983. The story of the White Rose, as told by one of Sophie and Hans

Scholl's sisters. This book was originally published in 1952 and intended for former Hitler Youth members and other young people in Germany.

R. Conrad Stein, *Hitler Youth*. Chicago: Childrens Press, 1985. A discussion of the origin and growth of the Hitler Youth organization and its use in World War II.

Ellen Eichenwald Switzer, *How Democracy Failed*. New York: Atheneum, 1975. Switzer conducts interviews with German people to examine the attitudes and personal reasons why Germans allowed Hitler to come to power in Nazi Germany. Includes a chapter on the White Rose.

Gregor Ziemer, *Education for Death: The Making of the Nazi*. London: Oxford University Press, 1941. Ziemer was the president of the American Colony School during the early years of the Third Reich. He obtained documentation that allowed him to observe National Socialist schools in action. This book is his account of his observations. It is an excellent primary source, and Ziemer's writing style is easily accessible to young adult readers.

Websites

Talk Origins (www.talkorigins.org) This website is a newsgroup in which most discussions center on the creation/evolution controversy. The archive exists primarily to provide mainstream scientific responses to the many frequently asked questions (FAQs) and frequently rebutted assertions. This site was very useful in clarifying evolutionary theory.

The White Rose (http://members.aol.com/weiberose). An excellent place to learn more about the White Rose resistance group. This website is an archive that contains all leaflets in both German and English as well as histories of the group members and the group.

Works Consulted

Books

Norman H. Baynes, *The Speeches of Adolf Hitler: April 1922–August 1939*. Vol. 1. London: Oxford University Press, 1942. A two-volume collection of Hitler's early speeches, translated by the author. This volume contains a special section dealing with Hitler's speeches to youth.

Howard Becker, *German Youth: Bond or Free*. London: Kegan Paul, Trench, Truener, 1946. A discussion of the ways in which the German youth was wooed by the National Socialists. Contains an interesting examination of the ways the Nazis made their ideology into a religion with fanatic young followers, who followed it to their death.

Richard Bessel, ed., *Life in the Third Reich*. Oxford: Oxford University Press, 1987. This is a collection of essays by various authors pertaining to life in Nazi Germany. Includes Detlev Peukert's essay, "Youth in the Third Reich."

Gilmer W. Blackburn, *Education in the Third Reich: Race and History in Nazi Textbooks*. Albany: State University of New York Press, 1985. An examination of the textbooks written and used in German schools to indoctrinate German boys and girls. It also includes an essential discussion and in-depth look into the way the Nazis conceptualized history and believed it should be taught to (and used to convert) the young people of Germany.

Harwood L. Childs, trans., *The Nazi Primer: Official Handbook for Schooling the Hitler Youth*. New York: Harper & Brothers, 1938. A translated version of the handbook given to each Hitler Youth member. Boys and girls were asked to memorize it and were quizzed on its contents.

Education in Nazi Germany. London: Kulturkampf Association, 1938. A pamphlet written by two English investigators about education in the Third Reich. It warns of the progressive militarization of Nazi education.

Richard Grunberger, *A Social History of the Third Reich*. London: Weidenfeld and Nicolson, 1971. An excellent social history. It cites a variety of sources that give the reader a real sense of the zeitgeist of Nazi Germany.

Alfons Heck, *The Burden of Hitler's Legacy*. Frederick, CO: Renaissance House, 1988. The story of the Third Reich through the eyes of a fanatic Hitler Youth leader as well as his discussion of the painful de-Nazification process.

———, *Child of Hitler: Germany in the Days When God Wore a Swastika*. Frederick, CO: Renaissance House, 1985. An autobiographical account of a former Hitler Youth who now spends his time working against hatred.

Jost Hermand, *A Hitler Youth in Poland: The Nazis' Program for Evacuating Children During World War II*. Evanston, IL: Northwestern University Press, 1997. Hermand's recollections of life in a variety of KLV camps. The book is fairly easy to read, but be warned, it contains some very explicit sexual content.

Adolf Hitler, *Mein Kampf*. New York: Reynal & Hitchcock, 1939. An excellent English edition of Hitler's book, the annotations by editor John Chamberlain are quite useful, and the organization and index make it more accessible than other editions.

International Military Tribunal, *Trial of the Major War Criminals Before the International Military Tribunal*. Vol. 14. Nuremberg: International Military Tribunal, 1948. One of twenty-six volumes of extensive documentation of the trials, verdicts, and sentencing of Nazi War criminals by an international tribunal following Germany's defeat and the end of World War II. This volume contains the trial of Baldur von Schirach.

George Frederick Kneller, *The Education Philosophy of National Socialism*. New Haven, CT: Yale University Press, 1941. A critique of the National Socialist educational system by a U.S. citizen.

H. W. Koch, *The Hitler Youth: Origins and Development, 1922–45*. New York: Stein and Day, 1976. The most complete history of the Hitler Youth organization from its inception. The author includes political, social, and military history of the organization.

Claudia Koonz, *Mothers in the Fatherland: Women, the Family, and Nazi Politics*. New York: St. Martin's, 1987. An excellent and extensive account of the role of women in the Third Reich, including a discussion of a variety of factors that influenced their participation: gender, religion, perceived race, and a woman's classification as genetically desirable or undesirable. Koonz's writing style provides an accessible and important view of the lives of women in Nazi Germany.

Marianne MacKinnon, *The Naked Years: Growing Up in Nazi Germany*. London: Chatto & Windus, 1987. MacKinnon's account of her childhood during the Third Reich includes membership in the Hitler Youth.

Erika Mann, *School for Barbarians: Education Under the Nazis*. New York: Modern Age, 1938. An account of the Nazi school system. The book is written to drive others to action against the Nazis and gives both factual and fictional accounts of life in the National Socialist schools.

Melita Maschmann, *Account Rendered: A Dossier on My Former Self*. London: Abelyard-Schuman, 1965. The memoirs of Maschmann, a high-ranking BdM leader, written as a letter to a childhood Jewish friend.

Ilse McKee, *Tomorrow the World*. London: J. M. Dent & Sons, 1960. A former Hitler Youth member's retelling of her childhood experiences during the Nazi regime.

George L. Mosse, *Nazi Culture: Intellectual, Cultural, and Social Life in the Third Reich*. New York: Grosset & Dunlap, 1966. An excellent documentary history of the Third Reich, complete with some interpretation by Mosse, a renowned historian of fascism, especially German.

Jeremy Noakes and Geoffrey Pridham, eds., *Documents on Nazism, 1919–1945*. New York: Viking, 1975. An earlier, shorter version of their multivolume primary document series. This book contains a few documents that were not reprinted in the multivolume set.

———, *Nazism, 1919–1945: A Documentary Reader*. Vol. 2. *State, Economy, and Society*. Exeter, Devon, UK: University of Exeter Press, 1984. Noakes and Pridham expanded their earlier work into a multiple-volume set of primary documents. This is the most extensive collection of translated primary sources in English.

Jeremy Noakes, *Nazism, 1919–1945: A Documentary Reader*. Vol. 4. *The German Home Front in World War II*. Exeter, Devon, England: University of Exeter Press, 1998. A volume of documents about the home front in Germany. Contains excellent information on the KLV.

Alison Owings, *Frauen: German Women Recall the Third Reich*. New Brunswick, NJ: Rutgers University Press, 1993. This is a marvelous oral history, a collection of Owings's interviews conducted in the 1980s with Aryan German women who lived through the Third Reich and World War II.

Lisa Pine, *Nazi Family Policy, 1933–1945*. Oxford: Berg, 1997. Discusses and documents the Nazi policy towards "ideal" families as well as Jewish families and those considered "asocial" in the Third Reich.

Gerhard Rempel, *Hitler's Children: The Hitler Youth and the SS*. Chapel Hill: University of North Carolina Press, 1989. A discussion of the ever-increasing influence of the SS on the Hitler Youth organization during the Third Reich.

Joachim von Ribbentrop, ed., *Germany Speaks*. London: Thornton Butterworth, 1938. Von Ribbentrop was the Reich minister of foreign affairs beginning in 1938. In this book, he collected essays of various influential National Socialist leaders. The book contains an essay by Bernhard Rust, the minister of science, education, and popular enlightenment.

Baldur von Schirach, *Die Hitler Jungend: Idee und Gestalt*. Leipzig: Roehler & Umelang, 1934. Schirach's (*Reichsjungendführer*) book is something of a propaganda piece to draw youth into his organization. It is a description of the ideology, formations and purpose of the Hitler Youth. It is written in German.

Louis L. Snyder, *Encyclopedia of the Third Reich*. New York: McGraw-Hill, 1976. An encyclopedia of people, organizations, and important events in the Third Reich.

Louis L. Snyder, ed., *Hitler's Third Reich: A Documentary History*. Chicago: Nelson-Hall, 1981. Contains a variety of primary documents (translated into English) important in the history of the National Socialists' rise to, and seizure of, power in Germany. Includes some documents from the Treaty of Versailles and relating to the Weimar Republic.

Peter D. Stachura, *The German Youth Movement, 1900–1945: An Interpretative and Documentary History*. New York: St. Martin's, 1981. Gives an overview of youth movements in the first half of the twentieth century in Germany, including the Hitler Youth. Also contains a small collection of primary documents that are very interesting and otherwise difficult to find in translation.

Johannes Steinhoff, Peter Pechel, and Dennis Showalter, eds., *Voices from the Third Reich: An Oral History*. Washington, DC: Regnery Gateway, 1989. An oral history that includes 157 "witnesses" that lived through the Third Reich. It includes recollections of a variety of famous journalists and politicians from both sides—victims and perpetrators—of Nazi Germany. It also contains the accounts of many men and women who were children in Nazi Germany. Some accounts are easily accessible for young adult readers.

Periodicals and Essays

Jay W. Baird, "From Berlin to Neubabelsberg: Nazi Film Propaganda and *Hitler Youth Quex*," *Journal of Contemporary History*, July 1983.

Agnes Dunker, "March 12, 1935," *Living Age*, September 1936.

Heinrich Fraenkel, "Is Hitler Youth Curable?" *New Republic*, September 18, 1944.

Stefan Heym, "Youth in Hitler's Reich," *Nation*, June 27, 1936.

Robert L. H. Hiller, "German Youth Will Gladly Die," *Survey Graphic*, February 1941.

Peter J. Hovenier, "The Education of a Loyal Nazi," *Social Education*, October 1983.

New York Times, "German Army Attacks Poland; Cities Bombed, Port Blockaded; Danzig Is Accepted into Reich," September 1, 1939.

Karl O. Paetel, "Nazis Under Twenty-One, Part I," *Nation*, April 1, 1944.

———, "Nazis Under Twenty-One, Part II," *Nation*, April 8, 1944.

Schwarze Korps, "The Triumph of German Youth," *Living Age*, August 1940.

William L. Shirer, "'Mercy Deaths' in Germany: Condensed from 'Berlin Diary,'" *Reader's Digest*, June 1941.

Frederic Sondern Jr., "Thousand-Year Reich," *Reader's Digest*, September 1939.

Michael Straight, "Germany Executes Her 'Unfit,'" *New Republic*, May 5, 1941.

Film

Leni Riefenstahl, *Triumph des Willens: das Dokument vom Reichsparteitag, 1934*. Translated as *Triumph of the Will*, this film was commissioned by Adolf Hitler as the official record of the Nuremberg party rally of 1934. It shows troops of Hitler Youth at play as well as many other Nazi formations. It is the ultimate piece of Nazi propaganda. It also contains speeches by other prominent Nazi Party members.

Index

on Adolf Hitler Schools, 65
Probst, Christoph
White Rose and, 75, 80
Protestant Church
conflicts with Hitler Youth,
54–58

racism, 14, 25–35
see also anti-Semitism
Rauhut, Karma
resistance movement, 72
on World War II, 90
Reader's Digest
on Holocaust, 34
on National Socialist
Schools, 45
Red Cross, 51
Reich Ministry of Justice, 73,
74
Reichstag (congress), 8
Roman Catholic Church, 56
Rust, Bernhard, 43
National Socialist Schools
and, 45

SA. *See* Storm Troopers
Sasowski, Margarete, 43–44
Schafts (groups), 42
Schmorell, Alexander
White Rose and, 75, 79–80
Schneider, Louis L.,
Nazi law and, 27
Scholl, Hans
White Rose and, 75, 76,
79–80
Scholl, Inge
on White Rose, 76, 79
Scholl, Sophie
White Rose and, 75, 76, 80
school, 43–51
boarding, 61–71
for boys, 49–50
for girls, 51
Schwarze Korps (SS publica-
tion)
war and, 85
Shirer, William L.
on Holocaust, 34
social Darwinism, 26
popularity of, 28

race war and, 25–26
*Social History of the Third Re-
ich* (Grunberger)
on family conflicts, 53
socialism, 15, 59
Hitler Youth and, 38–40
resistance movement and,
80
see also communism
Sondern, Frederic, Jr.
on National Socialist
Schools, 45
SS, 16, 33, 57
Germanization and, 69
Swing Youth and, 77
World War II and, 87
Stehkämper, Hugo
on Volkssturm, 88
Storm Troopers (SA), 16, 24,
45, 53, 59
Holocaust and, 33
World War II and, 85, 86
Streifendienst (secret police),
13
Survey Graphic
on strength, 31
survival of the fittest, 26
Swing Youth, 74, 75, 77, 80
Szapiro, Jerzy
on Germany attacking
Poland, 83

Third Reich
beginning of, 8
girls and, 51
Jewish blood and, 54
National Socialist Schools
and, 46
Nazism as a religion in, 56,
57
negative eugenics and, 34
resistance and, 72, 80
World War II and, 81, 90, 91
Threepenny Opera, The
(Brecht), 35
Tomorrow the World (McKee)
on *Heimabende*, 41
treason, 72
Twelfth SS-Panzer Division,
86, 88

*Voices From the Third Reich:
An Oral History* (Steinhoff,
Pechel, Showalter)
on family conflicts, 55
on friendship between Jewish and non-Jewish
youths, 47
Volk (people of german blood),
38–40, 50, 59
Volkssturm (home guard), 88
von Schirach, Baldur, 15, 42
Adolf Hitler Schools and, 64
belief regarding parental
control, 17–18
Hitler fables and, 48
Law Concerning the Hitler
Youth and, 16
ostracism and, 21

Waffen-SS
World War II and, 87
War Service Cross I, 18
Weill, Kurt, 35
Werewolves, 91
White Rose and, 75–80
Wittenstein, Jurgen
White Rose and, 75–80
World War I, 39, 47, 55
Hitler and, 18
World War II, 8, 10, 11, 56
Germanization during, 35
Hitler Youth, 81–89
guilt after, 33
Holocaust and, 34
Japan as ally to Germany, 14
KLV and, 67–68

"Youth in Hitler's Reich"
(Heym), 59
"Youth in the Third Reich"
(Peukert), 10

Ziemer, Gregor
on denial of promotion to
HJ, 24
on National Socialist
Schools, 46, 50

Picture Credits

Cover photo: Corbis/Hulton-Deutsch Collection

AP/Wide World Photos, 23, 42, 58

Archive Photos, 68, 70

Archive Photos/Potter Collection, 17, 57

Archives of the Simon Wiesenthal Center, 54, 72

Brown Brothers, 26, 89

Corbis, 13, 19, 28, 30, 32, 44, 50, 62, 63, 66, 73, 77, 91

Corbis/Austrian Archives, 51

Corbis/Hulton-Deutsch Collection, 8, 29, 79, 84, 86

Corbis/David Lees, 76

FPG International, 20, 37, 40, 41, 49, 52, 64, 71, 82, 87

Illustrated London News/Archive Photos, 25

Imperial War Museum/Archive Photos, 12, 14

National Archives, 16

North Wind Picture Archives, 46

Joseph Paris Archives, 9, 48

Rijksintituut voor Oorlogsdocumentatie, courtesy of USHMM Photo Archives, 38

About the Author

Jennifer Keeley is a freelance writer and teacher who lives and works in Seattle, Washington. She graduated from Carleton College in 1996 with a degree in history and her teaching certificate. She has taught history and social studies in both the Seattle and Minneapolis public schools.